Mentoring Matters:

A Practical Guide to Learning-Focused Relationships

Laura Lipton
Bruce Wellman

with Carlette Humbard

Second Edition, February 2003
MiraVia, Sherman CT

The Road To Learning
www.miravia.com

Page layout and cover design by Michael Buckley

Mentoring Matters:
A Practical Guide to
Learning-Focused Relationships

by
Laura Lipton and Bruce Wellman
with Carlette Humbard

Permission for some materials in this book has been granted by the authors and/or publishers.

Permission for adaptation of materials from The stages of a teacher's first year. In M. Scherer (Ed.) *Better Beginnings: Supporting and Mentoring New Teachers*. ASCD: 19-23 © 1999 by Ellen Moir.

We apologize for any oversights in obtaining permissions and would be happy to rectify them in future printings.

MiraVia, LLC • 3 Lost Acre Trail • Sherman CT 06784   www.miravia.com

Copyright © 2003 by MiraVia, LLC
Second Edition, February 2003; August 2003; September 2004

Printed in the United States of America

LC Control Number 2002726651

ISBN 0-9665022-2-1   Softcover

Dedication

To teach is to learn. We dedicate this book to the inquisitive spirit and boundless energy of beginning teachers and their committed mentors, who work together to make schools richer places for children and adults.

Acknowledgments

The term mentor originated with Homer, who, in The Odyssey *tells of Odysseus, King of Ithaca. Upon leaving for battle in the Trojan War, Odysseus placed his son Telemachus in the care of Mentor, who served as a teacher and caregiver. In contemporary lexicon, the word "mentor" has become synonymous with a trusted advisor, friend, teacher and wise person.*

The mentors in our lives have been more than trusted advisors, friends and teachers. They have been role models who have given us a vision of how we might behave and who we might become as we grappled with the professional challenges of beginning teaching, beginning consulting, and beginning our present partnership.

The influence of respected colleagues has been so profound that it is not possible to separate our work in this guide from their contributions to it. This is especially true of two masters who helped to shape the professionals we are today, and without whose inspiration and support this book would not have been possible. Our special thanks and deepest affection go to Dr. Arthur Costa, a beacon of integrity, authenticity and self-directed learning; and to Dr. Robert Garmston, who embodies commitment, curiosity and joy in work and life. These two guiding lights illuminate our personal and professional pathways and continue to blaze new learning trails. As our mentors, they constantly support, challenge and facilitate our professional vision.

This second edition is the result of rich and multiple experiences and opportunities to share *Mentoring Matters* with skillful and committed educators throughout North America. We have learned much from teaching this content to new and experienced mentors and by working directly with others who are doing similar work.

Specifically, we would like to thank several colleagues who have moved our thinking forward and contributed to our learning: Barbara Lawson, for her keen insight and skillful observations of non-verbal nuance; Jeff Peltier, for his continual questions and unique perspective; and Susan Thompson, for her simultaneous attention to broad patterns and specific details of learning-focused practice.

L.L. & B.W.

Contents

continued

Contents
continued

Preface

Mentoring Matters: A Practical Guide to Learning-Focused Relationships

Debbie, a first year teacher in an urban school, finds herself counting the days until the end of the school year. Five of her students have limited proficiency with English and four more experience mild disabilities. Surrounding her is an unending stack of forms, student assessment data and the results from the first classroom observation by her principal. She reflects momentarily on her pre-service enthusiasm and her vision of being a teacher. Now she just wonders how to meet the differing needs of her students, complete the necessary paperwork, replenish the centers and activity stations scattered about her room and prepare to 'strengthen her pre-and post-assessment techniques' before next week's evaluation meeting.

John has been teaching for ten years in a neighboring system but now finds himself in a new school with new colleagues. The beginning of the school year has always been highlighted by renewing connections with colleagues and establishing relationships with a new class of students. What was once comfortable is now filled with anxiety and apprehension. John's knowledge and skills were well established in his previous environment, but now he feels the need to prove himself all over again. Adding to his anxiety is the need to relearn the processes for logistical and procedural matters such as; ordering materials, acquiring equipment, completing attendance forms, requesting leave, and last but not least, getting paid. What are the everyday routines for this school? Who is in charge of specific activities? It seems as though he is two people—sometimes an expert and sometimes a novice.

Anna, an experienced teacher, is beginning this school year with an additional responsibility. She is now a mentor for a beginning teacher in her school. Anna's first thoughts are of her own first year. She remembers feeling isolated, inadequate and unsure as she faced that first set of students. How can she ensure that her protégé's first experiences are different? She gets excited as possibilities and ideas begin to surface. That feeling soon turns to anxiety. Where should she start? Will she be able to solve all of the problems that will emerge? Will she have answers to all of the questions? Should she have all of the answers? How can she support her protégé and fulfill her own teaching duties? How will it all work?

Challenges of Beginning Teaching

FROM their first day on the job, brand new teachers are expected to perform essentially the same tasks as experienced veterans. The trial-by-fire method of casting novices into the fray of the classroom has been the traditional welcome into the teaching profession. However, there is an increasing body of literature, research and professional activity in the area of teacher induction. Both this research and current practice indicate clearly that mentoring is a critical component in welcoming new teachers into the profession and supporting continual improvement in practice.

New teachers often have a mistaken belief in the existence of a readily available package that can transform their classes into ideal learning environments. It is part of the mentor's role to debunk this myth and support novices in developing the capacity to make effective instructional choices, based on a variety of variables.

As early as 1986, Huling-Austin, Putnam, & Galvey-Hjornevik suggested that mentoring might be the most cost-effective means of nurturing novice teachers and keeping them in the profession. Statistics of flight from teaching vary from 10% to 50% during the first four years. Formal mentoring significantly reduces this percentage (Odell & Ferrarro, 1992).

Without the formal role of mentor to define the veteran-novice relationship, new teachers are reluctant to ask for help, fearing the perception of incompetence. Caring, experienced colleagues are reluctant to offer help, for fear of appearing to interfere. Unwittingly, this double-bind often increases the isolation felt by first year teachers. Even with the role definitions, establishing and maintaining a learning-focused mentoring relationship is challenging. Yet the rewards of welcoming and guiding a colleague into our practice are fulfilling for the mentor, and the teaching profession-at-large.

This guide is designed to support the initiation, development and maintenance of a fruitful, learning-focused experience for mentors and their protégés. It is filled with practical tips, specific strategies, and menus of ideas that correlate to the developing needs of the novice teacher.

Exploring Our Assumptions About Mentoring

Learning-focused mentoring programs begin with both a shared vision and the identification of underlying assumptions and beliefs. These beliefs are the initial building blocks supporting and influencing the structure and expectations of the mentoring program. The goals of collaborative, growth-oriented, learning-focused relationships are based on the following assumptions:

Induction is an investment in retention, integration and continual growth.

> The ways in which an organization initiates new members is an important aspect of its culture. Growth-oriented, learning-focused school cultures provide time and resources to welcome and nurture novices. While orientation and policy awareness are vital ingredients in an induction program, mentoring relationships are central to the success of developing and retaining effective practitioners. Mentoring creates cohesive and collaborative instructional teams, and establishes the norm of on-going learning about and from teaching.

Emotional safety is necessary to produce cognitive complexity.

Attending to the emotional, physical and intellectual environment of the mentoring relationship accelerates growth from novice to expert teaching. Mentors must construct a safe space, where verbal and nonverbal communication indicates full attention and high expectations, carefully balancing support and challenge. These components allow colleagues to share questions, concerns, information and skill gaps in confidential, supportive and productive interactions.

Mentoring relationships offer opportunity for reciprocal growth and learning.

Thoughtful conversations about educational practice establish forums for learning. Mentoring relationships provide opportunities for thinking out loud, sharing information, solving problems and creating novel approaches to working with students. The learning is reciprocal, adding renewal for experienced teachers and increased confidence for novices.

The central goal for mentoring programs is improved student learning.

Relationships that support beginning teachers must challenge them to examine instructional connections to student learning. Mentoring conversations provide a focus on internal and external data that are individually and collaboratively interpreted and translated into meaningful and thoughtful classroom activity.

A successful mentoring program will be integral to the implementation of other school and district initiatives.

Programs operating in isolation provide additional stress and management burdens to educators who are already struggling with time and resource issues. A mentoring program can and should work in concert with other initiatives. For example, information about instructional strategies may be framed within the context of content-specific learning initiatives already in place.

Four Benefits to Learning-Focused Mentoring

Mentoring offers multiple rewards, including the personal gains of renewal in working with a new practitioner, pride in contributing to a colleague's development and increased consciousness for mentors about their own instructional practice. Learning-focused mentors serve to:

Improve instructional performance.
Expert teachers are able to monitor the classroom and flexibily adjust their actions in-the-moment and over time. Interactions guided by principles of effective teaching, within a learning-focused relationship, heighten new teachers' attention to student learning and alleviate beginning concerns (Huling-Austin, 1990; Reiman, Bostick, Cooper & Lassiter, 1995).

Transfer the district policy, procedures and educational philosophy.
Systems function most effectively when each member understands the goals, expectations and operating values. Successful induction programs address the need for orienting the new teacher to the school system, school, curriculum and community (Reiman & Sprinthall, 1998). Mentors also embody and transmit both their own and the school district's professional values.

Frame the professional learning journey.
Teaching is a lifelong learning adventure. No one knows it all or completely masters this craft. Advancements in neurobiology and cognitive psychology will continue to stretch the science of learning (Sylwester, 2000). New technology, curriculum updates, and an ever-changing student population all contribute to the ongoing need for continued professional renewal. Mentors are powerful models for novice teachers as they describe their own learning goals and help protégés craft meaningful challenges of their own.

Promote norms of learning and collaboration.
In *Learning from Mentors*, the National Center for Research on Teacher Learning at Michigan State University (1999) highlights the opportunity to establish a 'culture of mentoring.' Defining characteristics of this culture include an emphasis on the application of theory into instructional practice and the use of collaborative processes to increase the knowledge base. Given the emerging needs of today's student population, whole school alignment towards improving performance is fundamental to success for all.

Defining the Protégé

In designing the mentor's role to meet the needs of the new teachers within the district, it is useful to define some differences in personnel. The key distinction is between teachers new to the profession and more experienced teachers changing assignments. Novice teachers require different kinds and levels of support than transitioning veterans.

Most literature in this area defines the induction period as the first three years of practice. Teachers who have classroom experience beyond three years, but have entered a new system, or a very different position in the same system, generally need information about, and orientation to, policy, facilities, procedures and programs. Connecting with a mentor can also assist in the smooth integration with existing faculty. Educators making a grade or subject area change may simply need an orientation to the materials, resources, schedules, and expectations of the new assignment.

While this guide has information and ideas to serve both groups, it is primarily designed to support mentors of novice, or beginning teachers.

The reader will please note that while we are aware that both men and women compose the ranks of expert professionals in mentoring roles, we have chosen to use feminine pronouns as a convenience of form throughout this book when referring to them.

What's Inside This Guide

Section One: **The Mentor's Role**
This section defines the mentor's role in a learning-focused relationship. It describes the importance of balancing support with challenge, along with ideas for facilitating professional vision. Within a description of the phases of first year teaching, the section offers ways to anticipate the needs of beginners. These suggestions are arranged in a simple month-by-month format.

Section Two: **Learning-Focused Interactions: A Continuum**
This section introduces three stances for learning-focused mentors, arrayed on a continuum from most to least directive. It offers ideas for providing information while developing self-reliance, as well as thoughts and methods for fostering collaborative and self-directed learning.

Section Three: **Maximizing Time and Attention**
This section offers structured templates to guide planning, reflection and problem-solving. It presents protocols, time-saving strategies and nonverbal tools for focusing attention and supporting learning. The section also offers tips for supporting protégés when it is difficult to meet in person.

Section Four: **Learning-Focused Verbal Tools**
This section describes and illustrates verbal tools for creating emotional safety and producing complex thinking. It provides scaffolds for developing mentoring skills, along with exercises for personal practice.

Section Five: **Facilitating Professional Vision: From Novice to Expert Teaching**
This section frames the journey from novice to expert teaching, articulating the major developmental differences between beginning and experienced teachers. It describes four lenses of expert teacher knowledge and offers mentors tips for supporting personal and professional growth for protégés throughout the developmental stages.

Section Six: **Strategies for Success**
This section offers practical tips and concrete strategies for supporting, challenging and facilitating a novice's professional vision. These strategies are organized by times of the year and level of commitment/ effort.

Section Seven: **Appendix**
This section includes rubrics for self-assessing the mentoring relationship, national standards for beginning teachers, ideas and processes for developing a teaching and learning portfolio and a host of FAQ's (Frequently Asked Questions).

Section Eight: **Structured Forms, Tools and Blacklines**
Ever practical, this section offers forms for reproduction, leaving more time for face-to-face mentor/protégé interactions.

Section Nine: **References and Resources**
Looking for more? This section includes a rich and varied list of print and on-line resources to support mentors in supporting their protégés.

This guide is filled with concrete ideas for accelerating the transition from novice to expert teaching through the mentoring process. Practical strategies are purposefully interwoven with the research base supporting their implementation; related sections, appendix resources and blackline masters are cross-referenced to enhance connection-making.

"New teachers quickly, but with no small amount of surprise, come to recognize that teaching is psychologically, intellectually and physically arduous. New teachers also believe that they already ought to know how to do things which they have never done before. Another characteristic of new teachers is the sense that there are easily developed, immediately available strategies that can be used to transform their classes into some ideal condition. These beliefs and perceptions reflect an underdeveloped conceptualization of the inherent complexities of teaching."

Murphy, Covin & Morey, 1990

Section *1*   The Mentor's Role

LEARNING-FOCUSED mentoring relationships make a significant emotional and intellectual difference in the induction experience for new teachers, as well as in their continuing professional practice. These clearly structured entries into the profession frame the learning journey from novice to expert teaching. Beginning teachers benefiting from skilled mentoring are more likely to:

- Increase their efficacy as instructional problem-solvers and decision-makers

- Engage in collaborative professional exchanges regarding improving practice

- Remain in the teaching profession

First and Foremost

For beginning teachers, the benefits of a mentoring experience include:

- *Increased efficacy as problem-solvers and decision-makers*

- *Higher engagement in collaborative exchanges*

- *Increased likelihood of remaining in teaching*

Who we are as mentors, how we mentor and what we mentor about are essential to meeting the current needs of beginning teachers. A central component in a learning-focused mentoring program is a clear understanding of the respective role and responsibilities of each participant. Framing a mentoring identity as one who builds capacity in others is a necessary first step. The most important function for mentors is to embrace a growth orientation, understanding that the work is to increase their colleague's effectiveness as professional problem-solvers and decision-makers.

This process begins with establishing and maintaining a learning focus within the relationship. In this way, each party shapes and understands the nature and expectations of the mentoring interactions. We build on the work of Laurent Daloz (1998), suggesting that a mentor's role within such a relationship is to balance three functions:

- Offering support

- Creating challenge

- Facilitating a professional vision

These functions can operate independently in specific situations, but in the greater context of the relationship they must be connected. Balancing these three elements energizes growth and learning. Support alone will provide comfort but may encourage complacency. Challenge without support may increase anxiety and fear of failure. Support and challenge without vision may leave us wandering on a journey looking only at the ground beneath us but not the road ahead.

Offering Support

Support for the new teacher occurs in four distinct categories: emotional, physical, instructional and institutional. Sometimes the novice needs a shoulder to cry on, a hug rewarding an especially exhilirating success and every range of emotional support in between. Often, the support is physical—perhaps tackling the room arrangement, moving desks and setting up learning centers, or creating a special bulletin board or wall display, or even carting books for a thematic unit from the local library. Institutional support includes guidelines for applying procedures and policies, or expert advice on certain processes. On the other hand, instructional support includes content area resources and practical professional suggestions based on current research and years of rich experience.

In a learning-focused relationship, mentors offer support by:

- Attending fully—respectfully listening when our partner needs to share concerns, frustrations, experiences and new ideas.

- Responding empathetically—acknowledging feelings and perhaps a sharing of concerns, frustrations and experiences.

- Creating a 'safe' space—attending to the verbal and nonverbal communications that establish rapport and support thinking.

- Reviewing schedules—coordinating pockets of time that may be devoted to addressing pressing personal or professional concerns.

- Offering resources—providing time, energy and materials to ease the difficult challenges beginners often face.

- Providing information—about the practices and policies of the school and district to facilitate the protégé's induction into the professional community; and about the craft of teaching to support the development of sound educational practice.

Support
- Emotional
- Physical
- Instructional
- Institutional

Instructional Support includes:
- Time management tips
- Instructional strategies
- Student assessment strategies
- Ideas for establishing management routines
- Curriculum design
- Lesson planning

Institutional Support includes:
- Staff evaluation procedures
- Resource acquisition procedures
- Expectations regarding before and after school monitoring duties
- Current local initiatives
- Leave or attendance policies

Creating Challenge

Challenge
- Goal-driven
- Data-focused
- Thought-provoking

In our experience, mentors devote most of their time to providing support, such as that described in the previous section. However, unless support is balanced with challenge, we rob new teachers of the opportunity to grow and learn. If our goal is to nurture independent, effective practitioners, then it is critical that novices take responsibility for their own practice.

Growth requires that beginners develop the capacity to apply and adapt expert information within the context of their own classrooms. This development includes making meaning of new information and experiences. This learning enables new teachers to apply, refine and create alternative strategies based on students' needs, curricular readiness and teacher values.

Skillful mentors balance the supportive aspects of the relationship with challenges that promote continual attention to improvement in practice. In a learning-focused relationship, challenge is created by:

- Structuring rigorous examination and analysis of practice by applying Planning and Reflecting Templates (see Section Three, Maximizing Time and Attention).

- Engaging in goal-setting, and continuing to have goal-driven conversations.

- Maintaining a focus on student learning, including assistance in analyzing student performance information and determining cause-effect relationships.

- Exploring samples of student work, considering the protégé's decisions and experiences and discussing both positive and negative results of instructional practice.

- Actively engaging protégés in problem-solving and decision-making by forming problem-solving partnerships, brainstorming options and generating solutions.

- Assisting in the identification and articulation of criteria for choices and consequences with think alouds and coaching sessions.

- Building connections between current theory and classroom practice.

- Constructing and conducting action research projects, building norms of experimentation and reflective practice.

Facilitating Professional Vision

For beginning teachers, it is often difficult to project past the most immediate experience. There are no reference points to use in envisioning student growth. There are no memories to surface to help see the year unfold. The day-to-day operation of a classroom is generally new territory for the novice, so it is often necessary to illuminate the learning pathways.

We don't learn to teach;
We learn from our teaching.

Facilitating a professional vision creates a lifelong learner engaged in continuous improvement. It creates a picture of sound educational practice and high expectations. It suggests that a teacher is also a learner and reminds us that we don't learn to teach; rather we learn from our teaching. Facilitating vision is cumulative and developmental.

In a learning-focused relationship, facilitating a professional vision is achieved by:

- Setting high, yet achievable, expectations for the novice teacher, considering sources such as the Interstate New Teachers Assessment and Support Consortium (INTASC) Beginning Teacher Standards (see Appendix) or local standards that define what effective teachers should know and be able to do.

- Assisting in the identification of learning outcomes for students that are broader than one lesson or unit.

- Painting the bigger picture of content integration; connecting subject areas with real world applications.

- Developing action plans, prioritizing tasks and identifying resources for achieving goals.

- Encouraging collaborative opportunities with the mentor, other novices, and within the faculty (e.g., committee work, interdisciplinary projects, grade or department level planning).

- Modeling a professional identity that exemplifies the best we know how to be.

Facilitating vision
- High expectations for self and students
- Lifelong learning
- Professional identity

Again, our continual attention to balancing support with challenge, with a vision that embodies the values of high expectations and lifelong learning, develops a colleague who can exceed the rigorous standards and meet the difficult demands of professional life.

Recognizing and Meeting the Needs of Beginning Teachers

Beginning teachers' needs vary widely, as each novice brings a different perspective, experience, and knowledge base about teaching. Further, there are differences in preferred methods of problem-solving, learning styles, and educational philosophies. However, there are some generalizations that can be made about the needs, expectations and emotional phases during the first year of teaching.

In a study conducted by Simon Veenman (1984), more than one thousand preservice teachers ranked their concerns before entering the classroom for the first time. The perceived needs of these novices are consistent with other research studies on beginning teacher concerns (Bullough, 1989; Odell, 1986; Covert, et.al., 1991). These studies identify concerns about students; controlling and managing, motivating, evaluating, and differentiating instruction. They also point to concerns about managing time; for planning, scheduling, completing work load and balancing personal and professional life. Other concerns include relations with colleagues, administrators and parents. As we might imagine, beginning teachers worry about knowing what to do, when to do it and whether or not they will do it well.

Phases of First Year Teaching

Ellen Moir, Director of the New Teacher Center at the University of California, Santa Cruz and her colleagues, have identified a series of mental and emotional challenges that occur in developmental phases across the first year of practice. They note that while every new teacher does not go through this exact sequence, these generalizations are a useful map for predicting and responding to the needs of novices. The six phases described in their work are; Anticipation, Survival, Disillusionment, Rejuvenation, Reflection and Anticipation (Moir, 1999).

For novices, it is useful to understand that these phases are likely to occur as a normal part of their first year in teaching. As mentors, awareness of and sensitivity to these phases helps us to maintain a developmentally appropriate balance of support and challenge while facilitating professional vision.

The following pages correlate these identified phases with some ideas for providing that balance as a learning-focused mentor.

Adapted from Moir, E. (1999). The stages of a teacher's first year. In M. Scherer (Ed). *A Better Beginning: Supporting and Mentoring New Teachers.* Alexandria, VA: ASCD

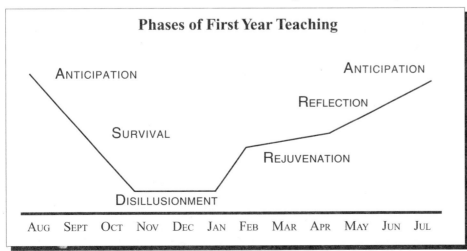

Phases of First Year Teaching

ANTICIPATION

ANTICIPATION

REFLECTION

SURVIVAL

REJUVENATION

DISILLUSIONMENT

AUG SEPT OCT NOV DEC JAN FEB MAR APR MAY JUN JUL

Anticipation

It is August and Janice is excited and anxious about the beginning of her first school year. She is confident of her knowledge and has a passion for making a difference in students' lives. She can't wait to set up her room and organize materials. It will definitely be different to have a classroom of her own.

New teachers begin to anticipate their first year of formal work during their student teaching experiences. They enter their classrooms with a commitment to making a difference and an often vague and idealistic sense of how to reach their goals. Major concerns at this time are setting up the classroom, locating teaching materials, establishing relationships with colleagues, support staff and administrators and establishing relationships with students and parents. The press of tasks and the emotional rush of new responsibilities often propel novices through their first weeks on the job.

• SUPPORT
Offer support during the Anticipation phase by providing information regarding materials, procedures, first day activities, and mandated paperwork for opening school. Set aside time to think out loud about your own strategies and rationales for room arrangements, first day activities, contact with parents and support services. Collaborative opportunities may present themselves as you jointly plan for the first day or week of school.

• CHALLENGE
Maintain a learning focus by having a goal-setting conversation. Establish some initial goals for learning and for the mentor-protégé relationship. Use national, state or district standards combined with the novice's assessment of needs (see Section Seven, Appendix) to be sure the goals are relevant and reasonable. Discuss ways that you will monitor your progress and celebrate your successes.

• FACILITATE VISION
Ask your protégé to articulate his or her idea of the ideal teacher. Share your own vision of professionalism. Expand the conversation to consider the ideal classroom and connect to the established goals. Remember to balance long-term thinking with support in the short-term. Assure your colleague that for now, it's fine to take it one day at a time.

Survival

It is Saturday night, September 30, and the realities of being a teacher are beginning to sink in. Janice is spending at least half of each weekend and most weeknights trying to keep up. She struggles with managing lesson plans, record-keeping, parent meetings and progress reports. She wonders if she really can do it.

The realities of the day-to-day work of the classroom soon bear down upon new teachers. They are faced with many different problems for the first time and have few of the routines and tricks-of-the-trade in their repertoires that help veteran teachers conserve time and energy. Most are running hard to stay in place and have little time for reflection or advanced planning. Many new teachers spend up to seventy hours a week on schoolwork. Often the core curriculum materials are unfamiliar and the novice teacher is only one or two lessons ahead of the class in preparation for future lessons. There is a constant need to learn the curriculum, develop instructional plans, learn and develop assessment systems, correct student work and develop and gather materials. Many novices do not accurately anticipate the amount of work their chosen profession requires, but most manage to maintain their energy and commitment to student learning during this phase.

• SUPPORT

Offer support during the survival phase by sharing materials and management tips. Time is precious and may not best be spent reinventing the wheel. Share tips for establishing routines and managing the activities of the day. Keep it learning-focused by thinking aloud about your choice points and purposes. You may wish to keep note cards handy during the day to record effective techniques that may be unconscious and automatized for you, but would be useful to share with your protégé. Attend fully and listen empathetically as frustrations and concerns arise. As appropriate, invite your protégé to observe in your classroom, or offer to model a lesson.

• CHALLENGE

Ask questions that help your protégé recognize effective choices. Offer your ideas as a menu. Ask your protégé to share thoughts about what might work best, and why. Gently challenge by asking your protégé to keep a structured Reflection Journal (see Section Eight, Structured Forms, Tools and Blacklines) and use the recording to focus your conversations.

• FACILITATE VISION

Celebrate the goals already achieved (or sub-sets of them) and set new ones. Have conversations about what drew you to teaching, what's been important and/or rewarding to you. Ask your protégé to talk about what made teaching an attractive career choice.

Disillusionment

Everything seems to be going wrong. Janice's evaluation observations did not go as she had planned. The experiments did not work, the students did not participate and she lost the supplemental handout for the integrating activity. Maybe she should never have taken this job, or even become a teacher. Maybe it is not too late to find another career.

After working seemingly nonstop for six to eight weeks, new teachers often 'hit-the-wall', entering a phase of disillusionment. This phase varies in intensity and duration as novice teachers begin to question their commitment, capability and self-worth. These factors, combined with fatigue, can weaken immune systems. It is not uncommon for new teachers to get sick at this time.

Several temporal events add to the tension and stress at this point. Back-to-school night arrives triggering stage fright and concerns about parents questioning both their competence and character. The first round of parent conferences soon follows with both time demands that cut into preparation for class and anxiety about relationships with parents. And the first formal evaluation by the principal occurs. Lack of familiarity with the process and, in some cases, the principal, adds to the stress load. Most often, the new teacher overprepares a 'showcase' lesson that consumes most of whatever planning time was available.

It is not uncommon for classroom management concerns and the needs of specific students to occupy much of the novice's attention. Routines and response patterns are not yet firmly established and mentors often find their counsel is sought and or required in these matters. Deeper issues of teaching and learning often have to wait until these issues are resolved or stabilized.

This phase is usually the toughest challenge the first year teacher has to overcome. Self-doubt and pressures from family members and friends complaining about the time that teaching seems to take away from their relationships add weight to the burden new teachers carry.

• SUPPORT
Continue to assist by sharing materials and tips for managing paperwork and conserving energy. Focus on what has been accomplished and learned to this point. Assist in the abandonment of unnecessary or ineffective routines and procedures. Collaborate by jointly planning for open house. Think aloud regarding parent conferences and first semester assessments and grading.

Acknowledge feelings of inadequacy without dismissing them by suggesting that they will just go away. Check in often and watch for cues from your protégé regarding needs. Assure your colleague that every educator experiences periods of disillusionment and everyone makes mistakes and feels insecurities.

Debunk the myth of professional certainty. Let your protégé know that you do not have all the right answers either, because there aren't any. Emphasize that there is best choice, based on best knowledge at the time, given the context of the situation.

• CHALLENGE

Create challenge by helping your protégé learn from experience. Coach thinking and support reflection. Collaborate on methods for refining practice. If the structured Reflection Journal seems burdensome, use quick forms to focus conversations (see Section Three, Maximizing Time and Attention). Pay close attention to signals that you're pushing beyond 'whelm' into overwhelm.

• FACILITATE VISION

Facilitate professional vision by calibrating existing state and expectations for a novice teacher with the desired state and goals to be accomplished by the end of the first year. Ask your protégé to identify some examples of growth thus far and share specific, concrete things you have observed. Continue to connect the protégé with other staff members, building a sense of community.

Rejuvenation

Wow! The job seems much more doable after two weeks away. Time away has allowed Janice to reconnect with friends, family and herself. As she reflected on the first half of her year, she was amazed at how much she had accomplished and learned. Beginning the second semester, routines are in place and her expectations much more realistic. Counting down to the end clearly shows she's made it through the first half, with summer vacation coming into view.

For teachers on a traditional calendar, the winter break marks a transition in the pace and flow of the school year. Time away with family and friends reminds new teachers of their life outside of the classroom. Rest and relaxation re-energizes body and soul. With new outlooks come a glimmer of perspective and an emerging sense that this is a learnable profession, one that with time and attention, can be mastered.

Many novice teachers return from break with a clearer understanding of the realities of their classroom, the system in which they work, and ways to access available resources. They begin to have a small sense of their accomplishments as well.

Confidence in routines and relationships increases as the novice automatizes patterns for behavior, time and instructional management. These, in turn, free time and energy for explorations of curriculum development, new teaching strategies and longer term planning.

This phase tends to last into the spring with a few bumps and surprises along the way. As the end of the year appears on the horizon, concerns emerge about getting everything covered and everything done. Worries often arise about students' academic performance and novices may question their own instructional competence.

• SUPPORT

Celebrate, share and mark goals achieved and milestones passed. Be proactive in helping your protégé begin to organize for the end of the school year.

• CHALLENGE

Continue to challenge by focusing on instructional outcomes and cause-effect results. Inquire about new learnings and applications. Assist in analyzing student outcomes. Seek collaborative opportunities to team-teach. Plan for professional development opportunities and mutually construct implementation and evaluation plans for trying out new ideas. Meet and discuss the results and learnings from implementation. Engage in conversation cycles of planning, observation/data collection and reflection.

• FACILITATE VISION

Collaborate with your protégé—plan a field trip or create a shared unit of instruction. Let your colleague take the lead, and follow his or her wise counsel. Try something new your protégé has suggested and ask for some coaching.

Reflection

Three weeks and counting! Janice recognizes the tremendous amount of growth she's experienced this year and feels pride in her accomplishments. As she thinks back, there are things she would never try again or would choose to do very differently. Next year will be exciting. She will not be the newest kid on the block and she has a workable plan for managing time and tasks. Janice also has greater comfort with content knowledge and setting expectations for students.

The last weeks of the first year are a time for reflecting and taking stock. Mentors support novice teachers by helping them to remember all they have learned, what worked, what was modified, what was set-aside, and to consider what might happen differently the following year.

End-of-the-year routines require time and energy at this phase. Parent communication, closing up the classroom and a mountain of paperwork demand attention to detail. For many, the emotional leave-taking from the first class or classes marks this moment in time.

• SUPPORT

Offer support during the reflective phase by providing information and tips regarding end-of-year paperwork. Share your routines for organizing end-of-year tasks. Make a gift pack of colored markers, tape and stickers for labeling boxes. Start a list of items to order for next year.

• CHALLENGE

Mediate a rigorous analysis and interpretation of student performance information. Facilitate reflection through learning-focused conversations; surfacing insights, applications, and goals for the coming year.

• FACILITATE VISION

Do a gap analysis. Make connections between what was expected, what was desired and what actually occurred. Explore student successes and mark the specific turning points for them and your protégé. Collaborate on constructing a professional growth plan for the coming year.

And Celebrate!

The Calendar of Options on the next few pages offers an array of ideas

for a learning-focused first year organized by phases of beginning

teaching, and research on the concerns of new teachers.

Calendar of Options

THIS calendar offers a menu of activities, correlated with time of school year, the developmental phases of beginning teachers, (Moir, 1999) and Frances Fuller's stages of concern. In her research with beginning teachers, Fuller (1969) defined the phases of concern as Self, Task, and Impact. Self concerns involve feelings of adequacy, questions of ability and potential effects on personal time and lifestyle; surfacing questions such as *"Can I do this?," "What might happen if I can't?," "What does this mean for me?"* Task involves management concerns such as scheduling, sources of materials, and many logistical issues, surfacing questions such as *"How long will this take?," "Where do I* find . . . ?," "Am I allowed to do this?"* Impact addresses concerns for others, including students, colleagues, and the school community. Questions that occur in this stage include *"How will this choice affect my students?," "What are some ways I could support my team?," "How can I improve on this plan?"*

It should be noted that these activities are provided as a menu of possibilities, and not a mandatory list. Activities marked with an *asterisk are described in detail in Section Six, Strategies for Success.

Phases	Concerns
Anticipation	Self

- Letter or phone call to make informal contact
- Informal get-acquainted meeting
- Joint Planning Session*
- Informal sharing of teaching materials, files, bulletin board displays, etc.
- Share Incredible Ideas Scrapbook*

AUGUST

At least two weeks prior to school beginning

Phases	Concerns
Anticipation	Self

- Share school plant layout, discipline policies, location and availability of resources/materials, etc.
- Clarify record-keeping/management procedures
- Check for readiness of texts, kits, equipment, etc.
- Begin a Collaborative Staff Development activity*
- Share a Welcome To . . . Basket*
- Schedule a Meet, Greet and Share*

AUGUST

Week prior to school

Calendar of Options   continued

SEPTEMBER
First Day of School

Phases	Concerns
Anticipation	Self

- Informal check-in and mutual sharing
- Have, or schedule, a New Teacher Luncheon/Shower*

SEPTEMBER
*Weeks One and
Two of School*

Phases	Concerns
Anticipation	Self

- Schedule conference times for: clarifications/questions/problem-solving around grouping issues, materials, and classroom management
- Apply the Planning Template (see Section Three, Maximizing Time and Attention) to a goal-setting conversation
- Think aloud regarding pre-assessment and uses of data
- Establish a basic contact schedule for first month
- Begin work on Professional Portfolios*
- Leave notes of encouragement in mail box

SEPTEMBER

Phases	Concerns
Anticipation moving toward Survival	Self

- Provide information/clarification regarding the local teacher evaluation policy, student progress reports and grading
- Share procedures and tips for Open House
- Review non-instructional duties (plan to accompany the first time)
- Think aloud regarding parent contacts and preparing for parent conferences, or offer an Idea Bank for organizing these meetings
- Portfolio Planning Meeting

Phases	Concerns
Survival	Self

- Joint planning for time management and new instructional units
- Discuss purchases and priorities for using any remaining funds
- Review teaching videos and discuss strategies/applications
- Protégé Support Group Meeting*
- Apply the Reflecting Template for a learning-focused conversation
- Emphasize personal, informal contacts

OCTOBER

Phases	Concerns
Disillusionment	Task (Management)

- Create some Lively Lifelines*
- Encourage contact and activities with colleagues
- Discuss impact of student extra-curricular activities
- Think aloud regarding student motivation
- Share personal time management strategies or offer an Idea Bank
- Schedule a Problem-Solving Partnership meeting*

NOVEMBER

Phases	Concerns
Disillusionment	Task (Management)

- Discuss pacing and curricular progress
- Calibrate overload and assist in determining priorities
- Provide information/clarification regarding end-of-course exams, grades and report cards
- Think aloud regarding goals for second semester
- Celebrate Success

DECEMBER

JANUARY

Phases	Concerns
Rejuvenation	Impact

- Mutual sharing of professional growth goals and strategies
- Joint planning for upcoming units
- Clarify schedules, recordkeeping, reporting, etc.
- Encourage collaborative opportunities with other colleagues
- Attend a professional development offering
- Portfolio Interim Support Team Meeting

FEBRUARY

Phases	Concerns
Rejuvenation	Impact

- Explore team teaching opportunities
- Think aloud regarding student performance data and its use
- Collaborate on an action research project
- Jointly structure student data collection
- Clarify/share information regarding final evaluations, schedules (spring break, student testing, etc.)

MARCH

Phases	Concerns
Rejuvenation	Impact

- Discuss curricular pacing
- Think aloud analyzing student performance data and exploring cause-effect relationships
- Provide information/clarification on student files/records, parent conferences, etc.

Phases	Concerns
Rejuvenation moving to Reflection	Impact

APRIL

- Mutually share progress on professional growth plans
- Discuss end-of-year schedules, final evaluations, student testing, field trips, etc.

Phases	Concerns
Reflection	Impact

MAY

- Schedule a reflecting conversation
- Identify successes
- Assist in analyzing student performance data and exploring cause-effect relationships
- Facilitate connection-making between personal learnings and application to future decisions
- Final check for clarification on parent contacts and reports

Phases	Concerns
Anticipation	Impact

JUNE

- Celebrate successes
- Think aloud regarding completion of recordkeeping and other end-of-year activities
- Presentation of Portfolio
- Share the load while Packing Up*

Section *2* **Learning-Focused Interactions:
A Continuum**

MENTORS continually attend to relationship and learning as closely entwined goals of the mentoring process. Skillful mentors intentionally provide challenge, as well as emotional and cognitive support, for protégés. They do so by helping their new colleagues develop identity as teachers, through an expanding technical knowledge base and enhanced instructional repertoire.

Skilled mentors support novices in learning from experience, helping them to calibrate future action with emerging insights. Fostering trust and attending to the relationship are critical to creating the emotional safety necessary for learning. Being clear about intention and behaving congruently signals a safe climate for thinking, risk-taking, and problem-solving. Our intention always is to create this climate while at the same time providing focus. Thus, the learning focus might involve planning, reflecting, exploring information, or engaging in problem-solving.

Intention-Driven Action

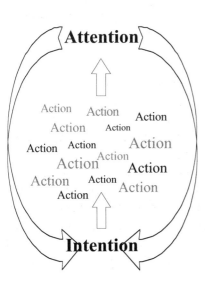

An environment, and a relationship, that is conducive to learning must provide emotional support for the complex cognitive tasks of examining and improving teaching practice. The choices we make and the actions we take are increasingly effective when they are consciously connected to clear intentions. Mindfulness of the intention to produce and support thoughtfulness about practice is an important function of a learning-focused relationship. Skillful mentors are conscious of this intention in their interactions with protégés.

When this intention is clear and present, mentors focus their full attention on cues from the protégé. They direct attention externally to signals from the protégé and internally to survey their own mental and emotional processes. The skillful mentor attends carefully to the external cues, both verbal and nonverbal, that signal a protégé's inner processes, both feeling and thinking. Intonation, gesture, facial expressions, posture and muscle tension, as well as specific things a colleague might say, provide a feedback loop for determining a mentoring stance, choosing an access point, and entering into the conversation and the protégé's world through skillful communication. The challenge for mentors is that this communication is interactive—driven by the responses of the protégé—and not a predetermined script.

For learning-focused mentors, this calibrating process operates both in the moment and over time. For example, during a reflecting conversation, a mentor notices her protégé appears to be anxious, so she chooses a supportive move, rather than a challenging question. In addition, paying attention over time creates a developmental perspective, rather than an episodic one. For example, as a mentor listens to her protégé describe a lesson plan, she is comparing previous descriptions and listening for indications of growth. Assuming there is increased precision and sophistication in the protégé's thinking, the mentor may choose to ask more challenging questions. However, if the planning conversation is vague and unclear, the mentor may choose to probe for specificity regarding student goals, learning outcomes and indicators of success.

Learning-focused mentors also monitor their own internal processes to calibrate, modify and align their actions with their intention to maintain relationship and produce learning. For example, a judgmental response might occur to a mentor listening to a protégé's description of a lesson plan. By attending to the reaction, the mentor has a decision point. In some instances, it might be useful not to share the judgment. In others, it might be helpful. The pattern we suggest to mentors is one of 'Whether, When and How': the first decision is *whether* to share the judgment at all. If the choice is yes, then the subsequent choices of *when* and *how* offer an array of possibilities that align with a learning-focused intention.

TABLE 2.1 DIMENSIONS OF ATTENTION

INTERNAL (ATTENDING TO SELF)	EXTERNAL (ATTENDING TO OTHER(S))

• body
  awareness of breathing
    patterns
  muscle tension
  posture, gesture
	• non-verbal cues
	  awareness of
	  breathing patterns
	  muscle tension
	  posture, gesture

• emotional state
  awareness of
  tension
  fatigue
  confusion
	• emotional state
	  awareness of
	  tension
	  fatigue
	  confusion
	  distress

• internal dialogue
  awareness of
  intention
  judgment
  stance
  choice points
	• linguistic elements
	  awareness of
	  intonation
	  inflection
	  word choice
	  metaphor

• toolkit
  use of pausing/silence
  intonation
  response patterns of
  pause, paraphrase,
  inquire or probe
	• content/context
	  listening for
	  problem frame
	  perception of issues and
	  perspectives

IN-THE-MOMENT (IMMEDIATE SITUATION)		OVER TIME (DEVELOPMENTAL LENS)
Attending to:		
CHANGES IN GOAL ORIENTATION		
from		*to*
isolated skills		clustered, nested outcomes
WAYS OF DESCRIBING CLASSROOM OBSERVATIONS		
from		*to*
• literal details		inferential reasoning
• individual ideas		categories
• specific events		generalizations and pattern recognition
SOURCES OF DECISION MAKING		
from		*to*
external guides		internal guidelines
TYPES OF QUESTIONS		
from		*to*
self-oriented concerns		curiosity about practice and principles
ELEMENTS OF RELATIONSHIP		
from		*to*
friendly associates		trusted colleagues

To maximize effectiveness, these choice points require that a mentor develop a wide repertoire of specific actions, as well as options for relating with protégés. We describe these options as stances and position them along a continuum—moving from most to least directive.

A Continuum of Learning-Focused Interaction

CONSULT • from the Latin 'consultare', meaning to give or take counsel. This moves beyond simple advice giving. To offer counsel as a mentor is to provide the 'why', 'what' and 'how' of your thinking.

COLLABORATE • from the Latin 'collaborare', meaning to work together. As a mentor, this means creating a space for true, shared idea generation and reflection with attention to one's own impulse control, so the protégé has room and an invitation to fully participate as an equal.

COACH • from the French 'coche', the German 'kutsche', and the Hungarian, 'kocsi', after Kocs, a town in Hungary where fine carriages were built. A mentor as a coach is a vehicle for transporting a valued colleague from one place to another. It is the protégé's journey. The mentor/coach is a guide and support system.

Skilled mentors operate across a continuum of interaction to support learning for their colleagues. Within learning-focused conversations, they flex between consulting, collaborating and coaching stances to develop their protégés' capacities to reflect upon practice, generate ideas and increase professional self-awareness. The ultimate aims of these interactions are to support self-directed learning by protégés and enhance their capacities for engaging in productive collegial relationships.

Versatility across this continuum supports response patterns that are developmentally and contextually appropriate for meeting the learning needs of novices. At times it may be most appropriate to consult; that is, to offer counsel and advice about processes, protocols, choices and actions. The mentor as consultant draws upon her own repertoire, experiences and expertise to advocate and offer perspectives and options. Alternatively, it may be most productive to collaborate; that is, to participate as equals in planning, reflecting and problem-solving. In this stance, the mentor and protégé share the work of idea generation and analysis. At other times, coaching, or the nonjudgmental mediation of thinking and decision-making, is the most productive option for supporting learning and growth.

In each stance, trust and rapport, as well as commonly defined goals and clarity of outcomes, are critical to success. Skillful application of communication patterns across the continuum of learning-focused interaction encourages the protégé to learn from and with a mentor, and to generate his or her own learning.

One way to think about these outcomes is to imagine the colleague you would like to have teaching next door to you. With this in mind, create a list of the knowledge, skills and dispositions of this ideal neighbor. Then, note the various approaches you might take to help your neighbor develop these resources. You will most likely find yourself crafting lists of ways to physically and emotionally support your protégé, ways to intellectually challenge your protégé, and ways to model and support a growing vision as a professional teacher.

Three Stances: Consulting, Collaborating, Coaching

Two major attributes define the stance a mentor is taking in any learning-focused conversation. One factor is the way in which information emerges during the exchange. The other factor is the source of any gap analysis regarding such elements as planned goals and actual outcomes or teacher actions and student behaviors. Within a consulting stance, the mentor produces or supplies the information and identifies and offers expert analysis of any gaps. Within a collaborative stance, the mentor and protégé share idea development and gap analysis. Finally, within a coaching stance, the protégé produces the information and analyzes the gaps as the mentor paraphrases and inquires to enlarge perspectives and clarify details.

To Consult

The intention of the consulting stance is to share vital information about policies and procedures, learning and learners, curriculum and content and standards and effective practices. The consulting mentor provides information in two important categories; information about how the district and school operates, and information about professional practice.

The first category includes the procedural expectations of the district and school, including legal and policy guidelines for matters like discipline and special education. In the consulting stance, the mentor might share information about policies for getting approval for and conducting fieldtrips, and how to manage bureaucratic tasks such as completing personnel forms and ordering materials.

The second category includes information about the craft of teaching including such things as; establishing classroom routines, developing a repertoire of instructional strategies and implementing curriculum guidelines. This information offers protégés opportunities for making informed choices and decisions as they implement these ideas and suggestions in their classrooms.

In addition to sharing technical information, the skilled mentor-as-consultant also shares principles of practice in the 'Why' of the actions and options. This intentional display of habits-of-mind models professional practice at its highest level and offers a vision of growth for the protégé. As protégés internalize principles of learning and teaching, these resources help them to develop approaches and solutions on their own.

Some Strategies to Use When Consulting

A useful template to guide mentoring practice is a pattern of sharing the 'What', 'Why' and 'How' of an idea or suggestion. For example, the mentor might say, "Here's what I pay attention to in situations like this; here's why that is important; and here are some ways to do it." The mentor then elaborates on the variables to be considered and the reasons for the final choice of action. When a mentor connects a specific

Some Strategies to Use When Consulting

- Think Aloud about your own 'What & Whys'
- Offer a Menu
- Produce an Idea Bank
- Conduct a Model (labeling the critical attributes)
- Review Tapes of Teaching
- Reference & Highlight Current Research

THINK ALOUD

strategy to the broader principles of best practice, the protégé learns to apply the principle as well as the individual idea. When a mentor shares the thinking process that leads to a solution, the protégé benefits from a deeper understanding of the process of problem-solving. Just as important, thinking aloud debunks the myth that experienced teachers have all the answers and no longer struggle with the complexity of decision-making.

Offer a Menu

If our intention in mentoring is to increase a colleague's capacity to make decisions, we must offer opportunity for decision-making. However, there are times when a novice has little experience to draw upon. At these times, it is useful to offer a menu of ideas; we suggest at least three. In this way, the protégé is still making a choice, but has the support of the mentor's experience. To increase the learning challenge, once a choice has been made, ask the protégé to elaborate upon the decision. The capacity to articulate the criteria for decision-making is a hallmark of expert problem-solvers.

Produce an Idea Bank

Similar to offering a menu, an Idea Bank also provides the support of the mentor's experience. However, while the menu is a spontaneous generation of suggestions, the Idea Bank is created proactively. In many cases, we can anticipate the needs of our protégés. For example, Idea Banks relating to establishing classroom routines will always be welcome early in the school year, or later on if management issues indicate the need for them. To keep it learning-focused, however, it is important to offer the Idea Bank when the protégé sees the need for it. Otherwise, it remains in the category of good advice that may or may not be appreciated or applied.

Conduct a Model

Demonstration is a powerful way to communicate effective practice. A model lesson conducted in the mentor or the protégé's classroom produces a clear example that is specific and tailored to the protégé's needs. The experience is more powerful when the mentor focuses the protégé's attention prior to the model. For example, ask a protégé to pay attention to the behavior management strategies, or the teacher's response choices, or whatever observable moves are relevant. Or, create a more formal observation strategy, such as a checklist or script tape for review and reflection after the lesson is completed.

Review Tapes of Teaching

Videotape is a medium for slowing down, rewinding and repeating very complex series of actions. Viewing a tape of masterful teaching offers an opportunity to closely examine effective practices. The tape might be one of many manufactured for learning purposes, or created at the school site for sharing specific instructional practices that are aligned with school goals. While viewing a tape from a consultative stance, mentors label the critical attributes that make the practices effective, or even stop the tape to focus the protégé's attention or ask for a prediction or cause-effect relationship before going on.

Referring to professional books and journals, or citing information from recent professional development offerings models the life-long learning journey of all learning-focused practitioners. This practice also plants seeds for a protégé's professional studies and grounds any suggestions that might be offered in concrete research.

To Collaborate

In a collaborating stance, the mentor and protégé co-develop the information pool. This is often the case once a problem has been framed or clarified and solution approaches appear. A collaborative interaction involves shared analysis, problem-solving, decision-making and reflection. The reciprocal nature of collaboration supports mutual learning, mutual growth and mutual respect. Each party participates, alternately listening, paraphrasing and inquiring towards shared understandings and productive outcomes. Ideas develop through brainstorming, elaboration, and exploration of external resources. Prioritization, evaluation and, ultimately, implementation might be the function of each colleague, or the one most involved with or responsible for the event or plan.

Some Strategies to Use When Collaborating

- Brainstorm
    Reasons
    Ideas
    Solutions
    Interventions
- Co-Plan
- Co-Teach
- Become Study Buddies
- Conduct Action Research
- Explore Case Studies

This stance usually arises spontaneously as an outgrowth of the mentor taking either a consulting or coaching stance to help frame a problem or planning task; or once a central issue emerges, during a reflecting conversation. Careful pausing and paraphrasing by the mentor opens up the emotional and thinking space in which this stance flourishes. The use of inclusive pronouns, such as 'us', 'our' and 'we' or 'we're' also sends a subtle invitation to the protégé to join this stance. After paraphrasing, "so we have a list of seven items to think about . . . ," the mentor can then shift to coaching or consulting based on her sense of which stance might be most appropriate.

Adopting a collaborative stance signals respect and the expectation of a collegial relationship. It is important to resist our own impulsivity to jump in and do the bulk of the analysis and thinking. Pausing to allow protégés time to think and prompting and encouraging idea production communicates our belief in their personal and professional capacities.

Some Strategies to Use When Collaborating

The most fundamental collaborative action is the mutual generation of information. Remaining nonjudgmental by applying the process of brainstorming keeps the exchange squarely in a collaborative stance. Among other things, we generate possible reasons or causes for a particular circumstance or event, a variety of ideas, potential solutions to a presenting problem or interventions that might be productive for an individual or group of students.

ENGAGE IN CO-PLANNING
AND CO-TEACHING

Working together to create a lesson or a unit of study, and extending that activity by teaching together are natural expressions of a collaborative relationship. As learning-focused mentors, however, we must be sure to include protégés fully in the process, creating a true collaboration.

BECOME STUDY BUDDIES

A mentor and protégé might become Study Buddies, choosing to learn together about a new instructional methodology or reading current articles on classroom related research. This common focus provides a launching point for creating new ideas and trying new strategies. The learning aspect is deepened when we identify and share feedback about our mutual experimentation and set new goals for learning and sharing.

DESIGN AND CONDUCT
ACTION RESEARCH

Extending a Study Buddy relationship into a more formal action research project deepens the learning potential and encourages a spirit of conscious curiosity about our practice. In addition, instilling a norm of experimentation early in a novice's career is a powerful way to facilitate a professional vision as a life-long learner.

EXPLORE CASE STUDIES

Case studies provide a context for dialogue about practice. The open-ended nature of most cases offers a practice arena to consider the complexities of teaching. Exploring a case study from a collaborative stance can be an intriguing learning experience for both partners.

To Coach

A coach supports a colleague's thinking, problem-solving and goal clarification. The outcomes of the coaching stance are to increase the protégé's expertise in planning, reflecting on practice, and instructional decision-making. We draw from the work of Arthur Costa and Robert Garmston (2002) whose model, Cognitive Coaching, defines this stance. Cognitive Coaching addresses the underlying thinking that drives the observable behaviors of teaching. With a focus on cognitive and related emotional operations, skillful coaches guide colleagues in accessing internal resources and developing capacities for self-directed learning.

Some Strategies to Use When Coaching

- Maintain a Nonjudgmental Stance

- Inquire . . . about
    Successes
    Concerns
    Whatever your
        colleague brings
        up

- Reflect on Goals

In a coaching stance, the mentor supports the protégé's idea production by inquiring, paraphrasing, pausing and probing for details. These inquiries are not focused solely on the 'What's and How's' of planned actions or past events. They also focus on the 'Whys' of choices, possibilities and connections. The intention is to continually enlarge the frame to take in a bigger and bigger picture as the protégé's professional confidence increases. The ultimate aim of this stance is to develop the internal resources of self-coaching for the protégé. Over time, the patterns of a mentor's inquiry within templates for planning, problem-solving and reflecting transfer to the protégé's inner voice so he or she can be guided by this professional self-talk.

Some Strategies to Use When Coaching

Coaching is, by definition, a nonjudgmental interaction. The only judgments are those made by the protégé as he or she plans, reflects, problem-solves and makes appropriate choices.

Ask about successes, concerns or whatever your colleague wants or needs to discuss, using open-ended questions designed to produce cognitive complexity. Questions with a wide response range encourage thinking and invite choice. (See more on inquiry in Section Four, Learning-Focused Verbal Tools.)

Engage in conversations focusing on the protégé's learning interests and goals. Interactions that are goal-directed will be relevant and rigorous, balancing support and challenge by marking successes and articulating new arenas for learning. (See more on reflective conversations in Section Three, Maximizing Time and Attention.)

Keep in mind that many strategies, including several of those described above, can be adjusted to align with each stance on the continuum. For example, student work samples can be explored from each of the three stances, depending upon the mentor's assessment of need. From a consultative stance, the mentor can point out what she notices or recognizes in a set of student's work, given her expert perspective. The conversation can move to a more collaborative stance by brainstorming strategies that would be most likely to produce particular qualities in student work. Or, she can shift to a coaching stance by asking the protégé to find similar examples in other student's work, or determine some cause-effect relationships regarding student performance.

Flexibility in Stance

Expert mentors listen for and note the ways in which protégés are framing problems and concerns. In general, they enter the conversation in a soft coaching stance, somewhere between collaborating and coaching. Until you know the other person's perception of the problem, you usually do not know which approach to take or what problem-solving resources the protégé is bringing to the table. Often, clarifying the question, in and of itself, is a major breakthrough and leads to insights for the protégé.

In a problem-solving situation, problem framing is as important as solution generation. If you continually jump to advice giving, it can build dependency and can, over time, establish a one-up, one-down relationship. Problem finding and problem clarification are hallmarks of expert thinking. Growth oriented mentors must remember to keep an eye on the bigger picture while responding to the issues and emotions of the present moment.

In a reflecting conversation, the perceptions and perspectives of the protégé are initially much more important than anything you think might have happened. This is true whether you were present for the event or not. If you have observed a lesson, this is especially so. Your comments, feedback or suggestions for improvement all need a context in which to be heard. The context always initially belongs to the protégé. It is, after all, the protégé's world and worldview you are entering.

Once an issue has been named and framed, the mentor must then choose the most appropriate stance for approaching the situation. This choice depends upon the knowledge, skills and emotional resources that the protégé brings to the situation. The choice also depends on the knowledge, skills and emotional resources of the mentor. Novice mentors often leap to advice giving because they lack repertoire for operating within the coaching and collaborating stances. They also often lack repertoire within the consulting stance, skipping over the problem framing and the naming of principles of practice, moving directly to "Here's how I do it."

If the protégé appears stumped and lacks repertoire for contributing ideas, the mentor then switches stances. As a consultant, the mentor might propose some ways to think about a problem or concern, offer options for action and then flex to a coaching stance to help the protégé consider and reflect upon the options and appropriate steps to take when clear choices emerge. By attending carefully to the protégé's thinking and own idea generation, a mentor can calibrate his or her actions and decide whether to remain in a coaching stance or flex to collaborating or back to consulting.

At other points, the mentor might be in a coaching or collaborating stance and it becomes obvious that the protégé is unable to generate ideas or options. The aware mentor then flexes to a consulting stance to produce information and perspectives. With this refined third point established, he or she can then slide back to collaborating or coaching; whichever is now most appropriate. This pattern of flexing across the continuum continues as needed throughout the conversation.

TABLE 2.3 A CONTINUUM OF INTERACTION

INTENTIONS	CONSULTING	COLLABORATING	COACHING
	To share information, advice and technical resources about policies and procedures; learning, learners, curriculum and content; and effective practices. To establish standards for professional practice.	To co-develop information, ideas, and approaches to problems. To model a collegial relationship as a standard for professional practice.	To support the protégé's idea production, instructional decision-making, and ability to reflect on practice. To increase the ability of the protégé to self-coach and become a self-directed learner.
ACTIONS	• Providing resource materials and references to research. • Demonstrating processes and procedures informally and through model lessons. • Offering a menu of options to consider. • Providing introductions to building and district resource people as needed. • Offering expert commentary on student work samples. • Sharing principles of practice by elaborating the 'What', 'Why' and 'How' of proposed ways of thinking about issues and proposed solutions. • Framing presenting problems within wider contexts and providing expert ways to approach issues and concerns. • Illuminating principles of practice that guide choices.	• Brainstorming ideas and options. • Co-planning and co-teaching lessons. • Sharing and exchanging resource materials. • Planning experiments to try simultaneously in each of your classrooms, and comparing notes on results. • Jointly analyzing student work samples. • Joining the protégé to offer support and 'translate' when building and district resource people are there to provide technical assistance. • Jointly noting problem frames and generating alternative ways to think about issues and concerns. • Alternating paraphrasing and summarizing oneself with encouraging the protégé to paraphrase and summarize developing ideas and understandings. • Alternating offering ideas with encouraging the protégé to contribute ideas.	• Maintaining a nonjudgmental stance with full attention to the emotional and mental processes of the protégé. • Inquiring, paraphrasing and probing for specificity to surface the protégé's perspectives, perceptions, issues and concerns. • Inquiring, paraphrasing and probing for specificity to support the protégé's planning, problem-solving and reflecting on practice. • Inquiring, paraphrasing and probing for specificity to support the protégé's analysis of student work samples. • Inquiring, paraphrasing and probing for specificity to increase the protégé's self-knowledge and awareness as a teacher and as a professional educator.

TABLE 2.3 *(CONTINUED)*

	CONSULTING	COLLABORATING	COACHING
C U E S	• Using a credible voice. • Sitting up straighter or leaning back a bit from the table. • Using the pronoun 'I' as in, "Here's how I think about issues like that" • Using bookmarking phrases for emphasis such as: "it's important to . . . ," "keep in mind that . . . ," "pay attention to . . ."	• Using a confident, approachable voice. • Sitting side-by-side, focused on the common problem. • Using the pronouns 'we' and 'us'. • Using phrases like, "Let's think about . . . ," "Let's generate . . . ," "How might we . . . ?"	• Using an approachable voice. • Attending fully and maintaining eye contact. • Using the pronoun 'you' as in, "So you're concerned about . . ." • When responding, using a pattern of pausing, paraphrasing and inquiring to open thinking; or probing for specificity to focus thinking. • Framing invitational questions to support thinking such as: "What might be some ways to . . . ?", "What are some options that you are considering?" and "What are some of the connections you are making between . . . ?"
C A U T I O N S	If overused, the consulting stance can build dependency on the mentor for problem-solving. Advice without explanation of the underlying choice points and guiding principles usually does not develop a protégé abilities to transfer learning to new settings or to generate novel solutions on their own.	Mentors need to carefully monitor their own actions when they enter the collaborative stance. Their own enthusiasm and excitement for the topic or issues may override the intention to co-create ideas and possibilities. False collaboration then becomes disguised consultation.	The coaching stance assumes that the other party has resources for idea generation. If this is not the case, pursuing this stance can lead to frustration on the part of protégés. You cannot coach out of someone what is not in them.

Mediational Mentoring: Establishing the Third Point

As a growth agent, a primary intention of learning-focused mentors is mediating another's thinking. Skillful mentors mediate a protégé's thinking first by establishing a focus for the conversation and then by applying their verbal and non-verbal toolkit to stimulate thinking. Mentors mediate thinking by asking open-ended questions, providing data, facilitating the acquisition of information, and strengthening cause-effect relationships, all the while moving their protégés towards increased confidence and self-reliance. We borrow the term mediating from the work of Reuven Feuerstein (1991), an Israeli psychologist who developed the concept of cognitive mediation. For mentors, cognitive mediation is a three-point interaction between the mentor (as mediator), the protégé and a focus, or third point. The third point can be external and observable or internal and referential. For example, external focus points might include a work product, such as a lesson plan, samples of student work, or observational data. It can involve a demonstration or the observation of an event, such as a model lesson, a videotape, or a specific student's behavior. The third point can also be referential, that is the focus is a reference to something that is not physically present, such as a description of a problem, an emotional state, or a perception of a student's behavior.

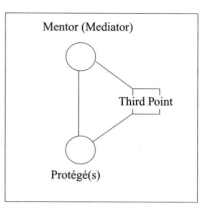

TABLE 2.2 PROVIDING A THIRD POINT: SOME EXAMPLES

INTERNAL	EXTERNAL
• A recollection or description • A personal observation • A statement of concern • A perception of a problem • A statement of value or belief • A judgment	• Samples of student work • Rubric defining excellence • A lesson plan • A curriculum guide • Standards descriptions (content, student work or effective teaching) • Test results • Individualized Education Plan(s) • Annual Reviews • Parent letters, communications

Mediation can occur prior to, during, and/or following any experience. Skillful mentors intentionally guide the protégé's experience, through questions, highlights and references. Mentors also use emphasis to clarify their purpose and importance, to sort significant principles or patterns from less significant details, and to create opportunities for their protoges to build and construct understanding.

Mentors facilitate thinking, or mediate, from any stance. Imagine, for instance, a mentor and protégé are meeting to discuss expository writing.

They are reviewing the protégé's fourth grade students' writing samples. The mentor enters the conversation in a coaching stance, focusing on one student's work.

> Mentor: *"What are some things you're noticing about this student's work as it compares to the writing standards?"*

> Protégé: *"Well, I think the writing has improved, but I'm not really sure whether it meets the standards or not."*

At this point, the mentor might take a consulting stance, sharing what she notices about the work and making specific references to the writing standards. She might then use a similar pattern with another student sample. In this way, the novice has several concrete examples that clarify and calibrate the standards as well a model of a more sophisticated lens for examining student writing. As they continue the conversation, the mentor might then shift to a more collaborative stance, suggesting that they brainstorm ideas for lessons that will help the all of the protégé's students increase their writing skills.

Mediating Non-Verbally

Physically referencing the third point in a space off to the side between the parties provides a psychologically safe place for information, concerns and problems. This subtle use of space and gesture depersonalizes ideas. It is now not the mentor's information or problem, the colleague's information or problem nor even 'our' information or problem. It is simply information or a problem about which and with which to think. Information placed as a third point frees the colleague to accept, modify or reject the idea as an idea. Without this subtle, but critical distancing, the protégé might feel trapped in a web of relationship and have difficulty freely accepting or rejecting the idea, for fear of hurt feelings. Thus, placement of the conversational focus creates a triangle, either literally or referentially, keeping the conversational container psychologically safe.

Nonverbal tools, such as posture, gesture and voice tone are all subtle indicators of the stance we are taking. In a consulting stance, the posture tends to be a bit more upright, leaning back slightly from the conversation. The mentor's voice tends to be less rhythmic and more credible with a narrower range of modulation than the coaching voice. This is the posture and voice of experience and wisdom. This is also the voice and stance that uses the pronoun 'I' as in "Here's how I've learned to think about issues like that."

In a collaborating stance, the posture is metaphorically and often physically side-by-side. The voice tone is collegial, approachably confident, with a blend of 'we' and 'you' pronoun types.

In a coaching stance, there is greater eye contact, closer proximity, leaning in and more rhythmic speech patterns. The voice is approachable and invitational. This is the posture and voice of inquiry, creating a psychologically safe space for thinking and reflecting. The dominant pronoun is 'you', as in "So you're noticing some patterns in your classroom that seem to be working."

Skillful mentors attend to the signals of their protégés to determine their choice of learning-focused stance. By attending to the protégé's verbal and nonverbal behaviors as they generate ideas and respond to inquiries, the aware mentor can calibrate the effectiveness of a given stance and know whether and when to move along the continuum. Our colleague, Barbara Lawson, suggests the following categories for organizing these important behavioral cues.

Learning-Focused Mentors Attend To:

THE LANGUAGE OF THE TEACHER'S GOALS FOR LESSONS AND UNITS. Do goals adhere strictly to the teachers' guide? Do they contain longer-term outcomes such as problem-solving skills, or the ability to write with an audience in mind? Does a given lesson connect to other lessons and larger contexts?

THE DETAILS AND LEVEL OF SOPHISTICATION OF STRATEGIES. How extensive and with what degree of nuance does the protégé understand the strategies to be employed? Is a given strategy option the only piece of repertoire that the protégé knows for a given situation, or is it one of a number of options to be considered?

THE DEPTH OF CONTENT KNOWLEDGE. How well does the protégé understand the knowledge, skills and concepts being explored by the lesson or unit being considered? To what degree does the protégé understand the connections between ideas in the curriculum? To what degree does the protégé understand and remember what preceeded and what follows a specific lesson?

THE ABILITY TO RECOGNIZE AND GENERATE CHOICE POINTS. To what degree is the protégé able to apply 'if-then' types of thinking during planning processes? How flexible is the teacher during lessons? Is the protégé willing and able to abandon or modify lesson plans that are not working productively? When reflecting, is the protégé able to reconsider choices and envision other possibilities and outcomes?

THE SOPHISTICATION AND DEPTH OF EVIDENCE AND DATA CITED. When planning and reflecting, how extensive are the student learning data upon which the protégé draws? Are data and student work used as a resource for planning and for reflecting on results? In what ways are the data being used?

THE LENGTH OF SENTENCES. What is the degree of elaboration of observations, strategy descriptions and reports of actions taken? How able is the protégé to describe thinking processes, choice points and outcomes?

THE VERBAL EMPHASIS. What words and phrases seem most important to the protégé? Are any words or phrases repeated?

THE NONVERBAL EMPHASIS. What gestures are used to emphasize key points in association with tonal emphasis and verbal repetition? Are any gestures repeated?

Versatility Matters

Expert mentoring requires a repertoire of knowledge and skills for engaging protégés in productive formal and informal conversations. These professional resources provide the foundation for operating along a continuum as we interact with colleagues. Having access to one's repertoire opens up possibilities for successful mentoring experiences and offers options for consideration when a given approach is not working. Knowing what we know and don't know helps us to identify gaps in our repertoire so we can consciously expand our own capacities as growth agents.

Versatility matters. In any given conversation, any one of the three stances may be appropriate. By reading the verbal and nonverbal cues of the colleague with whom we are engaged and responding accordingly, we can then flex along the continuum to support learning and growth. This flexibility in stance is the key to successful mentoring relationships. If our goal is to increase our protégé's capacities for self-direction, we need to continually offer opportunities to think, reflect and problem-solve within the flow of the real work of learning to teach. Our ability to continually anticipate, monitor and flex our stance across the continuum of interaction is a vital component in developing and maintaining learning-focused relationships.

Notes, Ideas, Applications

Section 3   Maximizing Time and Attention

FOR ALL of us—mentors and protégés alike—time may be our scarcest resource. In most cases, the challenge of developing and maintaining a learning-focused relationship exists outside of the expected activities and responsibilities of professional life. This chapter offers suggestions and strategies for time efficient, productive interactions. It begins with the most important use of time for learning-focused mentors: attending fully.

Attending Fully

Human beings are highly attuned to the nonverbal signals of others. We communicate our intention and degree of attention to others by our posture, degree of muscle tension, and how we respond verbally and nonverbally. We fully join the conversation and the relationship by aligning our body with that of another. This is especially important when the other person is ill-at-ease or when we are having difficulty understanding what is being said.

Ten minutes of our complete and focused attention is worth much more, in terms of maintaining a relationship and supporting learning, than thirty minutes with distractions. We actually maximize our time together by focusing our full attention on our protégé.

While our capacity to attend fully is an innate part of being human, there are times when the potential for distraction or lack of attention is high. For example, when we are fatigued or stressed our mind might wander away from the present moment, and away from our colleague. When we have a great deal to do, with little time available, the same conditions apply. Given the pressures of life in schools, conscious attention to being with our protégé is a challenge that is particularly important to overcome.

Communicating Our Attention

We signal our full attention nonverbally. Imagine you are in a restaurant, observing two people across the room. You can tell if they are relating well, even if you can't hear what they are saying. You might observe them leaning in towards each other, nodding, smiling, and gesturing animatedly as they engage in conversation. When we are aligned congruently with another individual, we are said to be in rapport.

Alignment has three distinct categories: physical, which includes muscle tension, posture and gesture; vocal, which includes intonation, pace and word choices; and breathing, which includes depth, duration and rate. As described above, we are in rapport when several of these elements are matching. Often, rapport is naturally present. However, we can intentionally create it by matching our colleague's use of these elements.

Alignment Categories

- Physical
    Muscle Tension
    Posture
    Gesture
- Vocal
    Intonation
    Pace
    Word Choice
- Breathing
    Depth
    Duration
    Rate

Being in rapport is a manifestation of our full attention to another. Generally, when we are fully focused on our protégé, rapport will be a natural part of the interaction. However, there are specific instances when we might pay particular attention to the use of rapport tools in our interactions (Costa & Garmston, 2002). These include times when we anticipate tension or anxiety or when tension or anxiety emerges within the conversation. For example, no matter how good the relationship between a mentor and protégé, there is likely to be some anxiety when we engage in a reflecting conversation about a classroom observation. Or preparing a protégé for a potentially stressful event like parent-teacher conferences or a first classroom observation by the principal is an important time to apply rapport elements.

Applying rapport tools is also useful when we are having difficulty understanding another person. Sometimes it feels like we're operating on different wavelengths. When miscommunication occurs, intentionally realigning and matching a colleague's nonverbals is often an effective strategy. A fourth occasion for intentional monitoring of alignment is when we are distracted or having difficulty paying attention. So often, the limited time we have to meet with a protégé is 'stolen' from time we would devote to other tasks. Sometimes it is difficult to keep these tasks, both personal and professional, from distracting us. In this case, intentional monitoring of alignment keeps our attention fully on our colleague.

Be Intentional When/If:

- You anticipate tension or anxiety

- Tension or anxiety emerges

- You are having difficulty understanding another person

- You are distracted

Blocks to Understanding

In addition to fluent application of the elements of rapport, listening with total attention, and without judgment, is a fundamental skill for mentors. In this way, we signal our support and establish a safe environment for thinking together. Further, we increase our capacity to understand and better serve our colleague.

To maintain this quality of listening, our attention must be on our protégé. However, there are several common internal distractions. These blocks to understanding shift our listening focus inward, to our own opinion or interest or surety about a solution. This shift to 'I' distracts from understanding. For learning-focused mentors it is particularly important to maintain awareness and listening discipline.

'I' Listening

Listening from our own world view diminishes our capacity to understand a protégé's perceptions and concerns. There are three specific categories of 'I' listening: personal referencing, personal curiosity, and personal certainty.

• Personal Referencing

Personal referencing is 'me too' or 'I would never' listening. It occurs when our minds shift from listening to understand another, to considering what is being said with reference to our own experiences and then judging its worth. This type of listening can be important in the consultant stance; but only after we're sure we understand our protégé's concerns, issues, and needs. Personal referencing often leads to judgmental responses.

• Personal Curiosity

Personal curiosity drives our listening when we are interested in what the protégé is saying, not to understand his or her needs, but because we want more information for ourselves. For example, a bright, young novice is talking about accessing the internet for a thematic unit on ecology. We find ourselves intrigued and want to know what websites are available, what type of hardware or software is necessary—and our questions are driven by our personal curiosity. While this type of listening can build relationship and is sometimes useful during the collaborative stance, it takes our attention away from our protégé.

• Personal Certainty

This listening block occurs when we are sure we know the solution to the problem, sometimes before we've listened enough to be sure that we understand the problem. Even before a problem is fully framed and mutually understood, this type of listening leads to offers of advice, or questions like "have you tried . . . ?" or "have you thought about . . . ?"

Giving our full attention to a colleague contributes to relationship and to clear communication. These are the foundations for mutual learning and future exploration. As consciousness about full attention develops into automaticity in our ways of listening, we can further maximize our opportunities for learning by using shared and specific structures for guiding our interactions.

Structured Conversations

Applying a shared and agreed upon structure to our conversations maximizes time, and also serves to focus attention by providing a scaffold for supporting and challenging thinking within a specified context. For example, when a mentor and protégé schedule an opportunity to plan a lesson, a structure for guiding the interaction offers topical focus and permission to keep the conversation moving. Further, a structure designed for planning increases rigor by highlighting the cognitive outcomes that support effective planning, such as predicting, envisioning and forecasting. This same notion applies to structure for reflecting and for problem-solving.

'I' Listening

Be aware of:

- Personal Referencing
- Personal Curiosity
- Personal Certainty

The conversation templates on the following pages are samples of efficient guides for purposeful interactions. They are based on fundamental and current theories of learning (see, for example, Bransford, Brown & Cocking, 1999; Marzano, 2000) that suggest the importance of specific intentions within a learning-focused interaction. The general template on the next page is based on the three phases in the Pathways Learning Model (Lipton & Wellman, 2000).

Each phase on the template serves a specific purpose. The Activating and Engaging phase establishes context and frames of reference. It activates prior knowledge and experience, surfacing the orientation and perception of the protégé regarding the topic at hand. It engages relationship, as well as mental and emotional awareness, and sets the scene for a thoughtful, learning-focused conversation. The Exploring and Discovering phase, whether in planning or reflecting, provides an opportunity for examining the details of specific events, making inferences and analyzing experiences; while the Organizing and Integrating phase supports generalizing from these explorations and bringing forward new learnings.

This general template can be tailored for specific purposes. The Planning Template that follows supports effective planning and problem-solving. Its counterpart, the Reflecting Template, is designed to elicit thoughtful reflection and produce transfer from one experience to many. Notice that these templates are designed to direct attention and focus on particular cognitive outcomes. For example, when planning, the mentor's paraphrasing and inquiry should cause the planner to predict, envision, and describe. While reflecting, the skillful mentor guides analysis, cause-effect and synthesis. Each of these structures guides thinking and produces inferences, hypotheses and new connections.

Versatility in stance is an integral part of applying the conversation templates on the pages that follow. While the questions are framed from a coaching stance, learning-focused mentors flex among the stances to support their protégés in producing the information and thinking processes within each phase of the template. For example, from a consultative stance within a planning conversation, the approach might include offering a menu of possible goals from which the novice can choose, modify or adapt. As a consultant, the mentor might also offer some possible success indicators for those goals. In a reflecting conversation, the mentor might encourage a collaborative stance and join the protégé in brainstorming a list of possible cause-effect connections between what occurred and the approaches and actions upon which the protégé is reflecting.

Specialized Applications for Conversation Templates

We propose the conversation templates as frameworks and not as recipes to be followed in a step-by-step fashion. The questions, within each phase, beneath each focus arena are intended as models and possibilities;

not as the only options. Different conversations will take on different flavors. Although these templates are relatively generic, thoughtful attention to their use for specialized functions produces powerful results.

What follows are some general tips and guidelines for applying the templates to different types of conversations.

GOAL-SETTING CONVERSATIONS

During the Activating and Engaging phase in a goal-setting conversation, it is important to take some time to clarify the roles, responsibilities and options available for both mentor and protégé. Defining the mentor's role initiates a partnership which can be shaped and negotiated to serve the learning needs of both members. Discussing the expectations of each partner reduces the possibility of disappointment or miscommunication down the road. Sharing information about the three stances makes it possible for a protégé to request a certain type of interaction, depending on needs. Use the template to keep notes and revisit the goal-setting conversation several times during the year.

Use the Exploring and Discovering phase to establish clear goals for the mentor-protégé relationship. Further, when a novice clearly articulates his or her own learning goals, the mentor can focus energy and resource on supporting the protégé in achieving them. Both types of clear, concrete and specific goal setting are important to the learning-focused relationship. The Planning Template is an effective structure for guiding these initial goal-setting conversations.

During the Organizing and Integrating phase, complete the goal-setting conversation by having your protégé summarize his or her understandings and name the next steps.

PLANNING CONVERSATIONS

Planning conversations offer fundamental learning opportunities for modeling and extending the intellectual habits of goal-driven thinking. Effective teachers set clear goals for their instruction, and identify specific systems for monitoring their achievement. They also generate contingencies should their initial planning prove unsuccessful during implementation. Attention to planning, and experience understanding the ways in which experts think about their plans, are important to the development of novice teachers. Applying the template for planning helps internalize important planning questions teachers must consider in order to produce high achievement learning for their students. Doing so with the support of a mentor increases a beginner's confidence and capacity for effective, independent instructional planning.

In the Activating and Engaging phase, establishing the context for the lesson or event allows the mentor and protégé to 'get in the room together', both the immediate space of moment-to-moment rapport and the conceptual space of the protégé's classroom. Experienced mentors preserve time for more elaborative thinking in the Exploring and Discovering phase by moving through this first phase as efficiently as possible.

The second phase, Exploring and Discovering, is where the bulk of the time is spent in a typical planning conversation. The four focus arenas are arranged in order of priority. This is especially important to emphasize to novice teachers, who tend to spend more of their time designing activities and approaches, and less of their time clarifying goals and success indicators. Reducing activity-driven planning is an important goal for learning-focused mentors.

The third phase, Organizing and Integrating, emerges from the general flow of the conversation. The focus arenas in this phase of the template offer options for extending awareness and producing higher order instructional thinking. Over time, skillful mentors note potential stretch arenas for their protégés and select focusing questions and/or suggestions within these arenas accordingly.

The Planning Template is also a useful scaffold for supporting problem-solving. Hallmarks of an expert problem-solver include the ability to envision the desired state and specify the outcomes of a viable solution. Skillful problem-solvers can also articulate criteria for and indicators of success. The Planning Template is designed to pursue these topics as they relate to the protégé's specific concerns. Again, learning-focused mentors can apply one or several stances to the problem-solving conversation, balancing support with challenge as they do so.

Problem-solving conversations can be scheduled or may arise spontaneously in hallway or staff lounge 'Gotta-minute?' moments. The Activating and Engaging phase takes on new light and new meaning in these conversations. Skilled mentors listen very carefully to the presenting issues and concerns of the protégé as well as to the perspectives and perceptions about the issues being described. Some problem-solving conversations accomplish the bulk of the work in this phase. By paraphrasing, inquiring, reframing issues and offering alternative frameworks, we model the habits of expert problem-solvers who spend more time clarifying and defining the problem than do novices. Novice problem-solvers often jump to solution thinking prematurely and spend time generating possible actions for ill-defined issues or concerns.

Once problems have been framed, the Exploring and Discovering phase proceeds very much like the planning conversation. Goals and success indicators are especially important to clarify. This process provides a reality check for the depth of the problem and for the qualities of possible best outcomes. Novices may need consultation help across this phase for especially tricky or complex problems. They may not have sufficient repertoire to generate effective strategies and/or know enough about situations like the one they are exploring to envision the array of options and choice points within the solution frame.

PROBLEM-SOLVING
CONVERSATIONS

During the Organizing and Integrating phase, the personal learning arena is often quite productive during problem-solving conversations. Again, experienced mentors note and mentally catalog the patterns of novice thinking in order to select the most productive focus arenas within this phase.

REFLECTING CONVERSATIONS

Reflecting conversations consolidate and extend professional thinking and habits of mind. They can occur after specific events such as lessons or meetings, or at scheduled intervals to reflect upon patterns of teaching practice and student learning. This process is especially useful at transition points in the curriculum, when unit topics switch; or at significant points in the school year, such as the close of marking periods.

Here again, the Activating and Engaging phase matters greatly. The protégé's issues and concerns and/or perspectives and perceptions are important to surface. Depending upon what emerges, the skilled mentor will select a stance to explore the protégé's current awareness. For example, if the novice notes some issues of concern and not others that the mentor deems equally important, the mentor-as-consultant may add these to the list of topics to explore during the Exploring and Discovering phase.

During the Exploring and Discovering phase, asking the protégé to weigh priorities is not only a respectful approach; but also provides a contextually sound assessment of the ways in which this novice is developing as a professional. Experts notice more than novices. By noting what the protégé is noticing and about what the protégé is concerned, the aware mentor can select an appropriate stance and help frame the content for reflection.

During the Organizing and Integrating phase, experienced mentors widen the conversation from immediate issues to the bigger picture. The connection making, generalizations, applications and personal learnings that emerge at this phase increase the likelihood of transfer of new awareness and insight. This is the true test of learning-focused conversations. Building habits of reflection and supporting transfer of and applications of learning is a critical responsibility for mentors.

Creating reflective practitioners is an important aspect of the mentor-protégé relationship. Formal, structured opportunities to do so make a powerful contribution to developing this disposition. Note that the Reflecting Template is designed to elicit personal discoveries, as well as new learning about teaching practice.

Learning-Focused Conversations

A Template for PLANNING and PROBLEM-SOLVING

ACTIVATING AND ENGAGING

CONTEXTUAL INFORMATION

• When thinking about this (lesson, presentation, issue, event), what are some of the dynamics that are influencing you?

INFORMATION ABOUT THE EVENT

• What are some of your questions and interests regarding this (lesson, presentation, issue, event)?

PRESENTING ISSUES/CONCERNS

• What are some of your concerns about this (lesson, presentation, issue, event)?

PERSPECTIVES AND PERCEPTIONS

• As we start to think about ____, what are some of the perspectives that will help us to see a fuller view?

ORGANIZING AND INTEGRATING

CONNECTIONS

• What are some ways that this experience fits within the larger picture for this year?

GENERALIZATIONS

• If you were going to give this (plan, issue, problem) a title, what might it be?

APPLICATIONS

• What do you want to be most aware of as you begin this (lesson, presentation, issue, event)?

PERSONAL LEARNING

• What are some learning goals for you that you might keep in mind during this experience?

EXPLORING AND DISCOVERING

GOALS AND OUTCOMES

• As you think about your (lesson, presentation, issue, event) what are some of the goals you have in mind?

INDICATORS AND EVIDENCE OF SUCCESS

• What are some things you anticipate you will see or hear as your goals are being achieved?

APPROACHES, STRATEGIES AND RESOURCES

• Given this opportunity to think through your plan, what are some actions you might take to ensure success?

POTENTIAL CHOICE POINTS AND CONCERNS

• What are some variables that might influence your actions and outcomes?

Learning-Focused Conversations

A Template for **REFLECTING**

ACTIVATING AND ENGAGING

CONTEXTUAL INFORMATION
- As you reflect on this event, what are some things that come to mind?

INFORMATION ABOUT THE EVENT
- What are some of the factors that influenced what happened?

PRESENTING ISSUES/CONCERNS
- Given your recollections, what are some of the things that capture your attention?

PERSPECTIVES AND PERCEPTIONS
- What are some of the things you are noticing about your own reactions to this event?

ORGANIZING AND INTEGRATING

CONNECTIONS
- What are some ways that this experience fits within the larger picture for this year?

GENERALIZATIONS
- Based on this experience, what advice would you give to someone about to do something similar?

APPLICATIONS
- What are some of the things that you are taking away from this experience that will influence your practice in the future?

PERSONAL LEARNING
- What are some of the things you are learning about (yourself, your students, this curriculum, this unit, this aspect of your teaching)?

EXPLORING AND DISCOVERING

WEIGH PRIORITIES
- Given your impressions, what might we focus on that will be most useful to you?

SEARCH FOR PATTERNS
- As you reflect on this event, what are some patterns of which you are aware?

COMPARE/CONTRAST
- How might you describe any differences between what you anticipated and what occurred?

ANALYZE CAUSE-EFFECT RELATIONSHIPS
- Choose one significant element in this event. What might have been some of the things that caused that?

Navigating Within and Across the Conversation Templates

We offer a metaphor of 'map' for the Conversation Templates. A map defines boundaries, clarifying what belongs inside and what is external to the territory. So, too, do these structures provide clarity about the parameters of the conversation. In this way, when used skillfully, they are especially time efficient, allowing either colleague to return to the agreed upon purpose(s) of the meeting. A map also can be shared, so both parties know what territory can be explored and what routes are possible—whether we take the same path each time, or vary it. Further, while each area on a map is clearly defined, we may choose to apportion our time visiting several neighborhoods, or spend most of it concentrated in one or two. In fact, once the mentor and protégé have had some experience with the Conversation Templates, they are rarely applied linearly. That is, moving from one arena (establishing goals and outcomes) to another (potential choice points) and then to a third (indicators of success) and then back to the first (for more goals and outcomes) is quite common. It also makes sense, frequently, to navigate across the templates—drawing from past experiences, or reflecting, while developing a plan. Or finishing a reflecting conversation with questions for applying new learning to a future plan.

Balancing Support with Challenge

As described above, the Planning and Reflecting Templates offer a structure to mentor-protégé conversations. These guides enhance the efficiency of meeting time by providing a shared focus. They also serve as learning scaffolds, allowing novices to internalize the thinking protocols that guide experts when they plan and reflect about their own practice. The questions and ways of thinking that are explored during structured conversations become an internal voice for novices when they are working independently.

As a result, after several applications of the Conversation Templates, the protégé comes to a planning or reflecting meeting prepared to respond to the challenging questions of the mentor. This readiness and confidence sets the stage for increasingly rigorous conversations about teaching practice and increasingly effective solutions to the inevitable challenges of classroom life.

Using Quick Forms

When the time, attention, or opportunity for a formal planning, reflecting, or problem-solving conversation is not available, there are other ways to facilitate a novice's thoughtful participation in learning-focused interactions. Practical and simply-structured protocols will save time and effectively balance support with challenge. Using these Quick Forms signals our expectations that, while we are very willing to provide support, we are not expecting to do all the thinking or problem-solving for our protégé. We consider these strategies to be scaffolds. That is, just as the construction metaphor suggests, they are structures to support a learner in reaching higher than they could without it. It also suggests that these scaffolds are temporary and adjustable, being moved where and when they are needed, and ultimately removed altogether. The three examples below require brief preparation prior to a scheduled meeting and can be applied in a variety of ways.

3 - 2 - 1

3 - 2 - 1 offers a structured approach for protégés to organize thinking and focus communication. The information can be written on an index card, or note pad. Or, if a protégé is keeping a log or journal, the 3-2-1 structure offers an effective format for entries. Because it is so versatile, we use 3-2-1 for planning, reflecting and problem-solving. For example, prior to planning, ask a protégé to jot down three possible goals for the lesson (or unit), two specific success indicators and one strategy that might be used. Or, at the end of class, after teaching a new strategy, ask for three things that were noticed about the students' learning, two surprises and one new understanding. As a problem-solving support, ask for three ways to think about the problem (or three perspectives on it), two potential contributing or causal factors, and one possible solution.

Asking a busy novice for six pieces of information makes the task doable while appropriately placing the responsibility for defining the problem or gathering the necessary information on the protégé.

STEM COMPLETIONS

Fill-ins, or stem completions, build confidence in responding to open-ended questions while honing a novice's thinking skills. Use the same stem completion regularly and consistently, for example, every Friday a protégé might fill-in the following:

> "The most interesting thing that happened this week was . . . " or, "One thing I'd never do the same way again is . . . " or, "This week, I was pleasantly surprised by . . . " or, "I discovered that . . . "

Or vary the stem to exercise and focus specific cognitive outcomes, such as comparison. For example, "Some things that are the same about teaching reading and teaching math are . . ." Stem completions also serve to facilitate professional vision. Generate stems that require articulation of values. For example, "The most important thing a teacher can do for struggling students is . . . " or "A priority for me as a learning-focused teacher is . . ."

Stem completions support and challenge thinking and provide a quick start for purposeful mentor-protégé interactions. They also develop the important habits of reflective, value-driven professional practice.

P+ M- I*

The P+ M- I*, or Plus, Minus, Interesting Frame, developed by Edward DeBono, supports reflection, self-assessment, and evaluative thinking. A three column sheet is used to record the Pluses, or positive aspects, of an event, plan or situation; the Minuses, or negative aspects; and the

Interesting or intriguing ideas that are neither plus nor minus. For example, a new teacher might do a P+ M- I* on a solution he or she is considering, or for a plan to try a new classroom management system. The P+ M- I* can be used to reflect upon a unit that was just completed or a recently conducted parent conference.

When You Can't Meet 'Face-to-Face'

There are times when it is difficult for mentors and protégés to schedule meeting time. However, this obstacle doesn't eliminate the need for on-going communication. We can maintain communication using some traditional and some novel methods to keep in touch. Of course, communicating by telephone or e-mail is one way to touch base without a formal meeting. Notes in the school mailbox and memos through district mail services are also channels for communication. To enhance these methods, get in the habit of using the 3-2-1, stem completions, P+ M- I* or other structures to facilitate clear, concise communication while exercising the important thinking skills these structures require.

In addition to those described above, use the following Quick Forms for enhancing mentor-protégé communication when meeting is not possible or must be delayed.

Taking a page from classroom-based literacy strategies, Double-Entry Journals also work well for mentors and protégés. The protégé enters a dated entry in the left hand column; the mentor responds in the right hand column and returns the journal to the protégé. This simple exchange can work to provide a quick tip in a timely fashion, increase a novice's confidence in a choice or decision, or offer the emotional support of knowing someone is connected and listening.

DOUBLE-ENTRY JOURNALS

A variation on the Double-Entry Journal, the Question of the Week has a similar format. That is, two columns are used; the left-hand columns are labeled by days of the week, the right hand column is for the mentor's response. The Questions of the Week strategy offers the novice a chance to ask a question at the end of each day, or on particular days when questions arise, and leave it at an agreed upon spot (e.g., in the mentor's mailbox, or on her desk). In many cases, the mentor then offers a quick response or resource or, if necessary, suggests a phone call or meeting.

QUESTIONS OF THE WEEK

The time frames for this strategy can be modified in many ways. For example, a Question of the Week could be a Friday ritual with the protégé looking forward to a response on Monday morning; or, change to Questions of the Month or Marking Period and so on.

MINDFUL MEMORANDUMS

The Mindful Memorandum has a priority gauge that directs the mentor's attention to the protégé's level of need. In addition, it requires concise, organized communication on whether the topic is an urgent problem or an interesting anecdote.

Mindful Memorandum   To: From: Date:

Hottest Topic of the Moment:

Questions/Concerns/Successes

Priority Gauge:		
☐ Need To Talk Now!	☐ When You Can, But Soon	☐ Whenever

Mentor's Response

To: From: Date:

Response/Comments:

Section  Learning-Focused Verbal Tools

RELATIONSHIP and learning are intertwined both in-the-moment and over time. Learning and thinking draw upon person-to-person and person-to-idea connections. These linkages require purposeful assembly. Subtle moves and behaviors nurture the mentoring relationship and desired thinking processes. Our consciousness of these components helps us to support productive outcomes. Inattention to these elements can hinder or block interpersonal and intellectual connection-making.

Applying Verbal Tools

The limits of my language mean the limits of my world.

Gloria Steinem

Language and thinking are interactive processes. Each energizes the other. Each limits the other. Learning-focused conversations create, nourish, and sustain language development. The ultimate goal of such conversations is to support language and thinking production capacities in our protégés. In the process, we often extend our own thinking and language production capacities.

How we interact with others matters as much as the content about which we interact. Thoughtful, thought-filled conversations require carefully constructed containers to support them. We craft these containers from several important verbal elements drawn from a learning-focused toolkit.

- **Pausing** to provide a space for thinking

- **Paraphrasing** to establish a relationship and increase understanding

- **Inquiring** to invite the construction of new connections and meanings

- **Probing** gently to clarify thinking and increase precision

- **Extending** thinking by providing resources and information

Providing Emotional Safety

The important linguistic moves listed above and elaborated upon in the following pages need careful packaging to achieve their ultimate and most powerful impacts within mentoring conversations. This package is shaped by several critical paralinguistic and linguistic structures. The prefix 'para' means above and around. In this case, the packaging elements are above and around the linguistic moves. These elements include such things as voice tone, inflection and pace. In other words, how we say what we say. Also, within the paraphrase and within the question forms of inquiring and probing, several language components influence the emotional and cognitive resources available in the moment to the protégé.

We call this packaging the invitation. We are, in fact, creating the emotional environment that invites our colleague to think with us. This notion builds upon current research in neurobiology which stresses the primacy of emotional processing and its direct links to higher cognitive processes. There are a greater number of neural fibers running from the brain's emotional centers up into logical/rational areas than there are running in the opposite direction (Sylwester, 2000).

Threat or perceived threat inhibits thinking. Our brains are wired to detect the subtleties of muscle tension, posture, gesture and vocal stresses that signal danger in any form. Incoming sensory data moves through biochemically driven switching centers in the limbic portion of the brain. Branching circuits direct the signals first to a structure called the amygdala, which scans, codes, and assesses the present experience for signs of danger. If the incoming information passes this test, another circuit fires and sends the message to the prefrontal lobes of the cortex for processing. If any threat is detected, this 'upshifting' is either inhibited or aborted. A classic example of this is watching a student panic and freeze when asked a question in class. The answer may be in his brain but it is not biochemically accessible in that instance. We must provide emotional safety in order to produce cognitive complexity.

Silence Can Be Golden

The pace of a conversation affects both the emotional and intellectual climate. Frequent, well-placed pauses contribute to a protégé's confidence and capacity. For most people, however, consciously pausing to provide a space for thinking requires patience and practice. Silence can feel uncomfortable. The fast pace of our world tends to support the belief that there is a relationship between speed and intelligence. However, complex thinking takes and requires time.

Using Wait Time

The mentor's intent in learning-focused interactions is to provide thoughtful paraphrases and questions that invite the protégé to think deeply and diversely. Patiently providing quiet time for uninterrupted thinking supports this intention and can be one of our greatest gifts to the novice.

• WAIT TIME I

Educator and researcher Mary Budd Rowe (1986) defined three types of pauses, or wait time. Wait Time I is the length of time we pause after asking a question. Rowe suggests three to five seconds. This pause allows time and signals support for thinking. It also communicates our belief in our colleague's capacity to think.

Pause to Enhance Thinking & Thoughtfulness

WAIT TIME I

PAUSE after asking a question

- to allow thinking time
- to signal support for thinking
- to demonstrate your belief in your colleague's capacity for thinking.

WAIT TIME II

PAUSE after a colleague responds

- to allow time to retrieve additional and / or related information

WAIT TIME III

PAUSE before your next question or response

- to model thoughtfulness and a need to think before responding

• Wait Time II

Wait Time II is the pause provided after a response has been given. The colleague is provided time to mentally retrieve additional and/or related information. A minimum of three seconds is recommended; however, higher level cognitive tasks may require five seconds or more.

• Wait Time III

Wait Time III is the length of time the mentor takes before responding. This type of pause communicates our own need to form language, models the importance of thinking before responding and displays value for thoughtfulness.

Communicating Meaning Through Physical Referencing

Physical Referencing

- Characters in space
- Concepts in space
- Sequence or hierarchy
- Time orientations

Further, in addition to silence, human beings have a rich repertoire of nonverbal expressions. The brain and the body are an integrated system. What is happening on the inside is reflected in sometimes subtle, and in other times overt ways by various parts of the body.

Individuals' nonverbal communication patterns are as rich and as distinctive as is their spoken language. People have unique external cues to their internal thinking processes. Handedness plays a part in these patterns. Discerning hand dominance and observing marker cues is a useful communication tool. By noting where in space a colleague places story elements and characters, we can paraphrase both verbally and nonverbally by referencing these locations with our own gestures.

Language is not an innocent reflection of how we think. The terms we use control our perceptions, shape our understandings, and lead us to particular proposals for improvement. We can see only as far as our language allows us to see.

Martin Haberman

This subtle, but powerful skill communicates safety and mediates thinking. Pay attention to which hand holds which character or characters in the 'story' being told, and reflect these elements when engaging with a colleague. By paying attention to these elements as they are communicated, an observant mentor facilitates communication and accelerates learning.

Inviting Thinking

Elements of the Invitation

The invitation to think functions as a total package wrapped around our paraphrases and our questions. In Section Three, Maximizing Time and Attention, we explored patterns of attending fully. By applying the elements of rapport, we signal that our full presence is available for this conversation and that we intend no harm. To these tools we add several important verbal patterns that invite thinking.

• APPROACHABLE VOICE

The first verbal element in the invitation to think is the use of an approachable voice for framing our own language in a nonthreatening manner. We learned this pattern from Michael Grinder, a classroom management expert and specialist in nonverbal patterns of communication (Grinder, 1995). An *approachable voice* is well modulated and tends to rise at the end of the statement, paraphrase or question, signaling openness and exploration. This intonation contrasts with the *credible voice* which is more evenly modulated and tends to drop at the end of a statement. Voice choice also signals the stance within which we are operating. The more approachable voice indicates a coaching stance; the more credible voice a consulting stance.

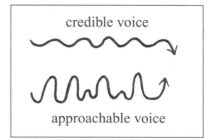

• PLURAL FORMS

Two key syntactical choices make it emotionally easier for the protégé to think and increase the options for thinking. The first is to use plural forms: *goals* instead *goal*, *concerns* rather than *concern*. This pattern frees the protégé from having to evaluate and sort at this point in the conversation. Some people need to hear their issues aloud before they know which are most central.

Inviting Thinking
- Attending Fully
- Approachable Voice
- Plural Forms
- Exploratory Language
- Positive Presupposition

• EXPLORATORY LANGUAGE

The second language move is to use exploratory phrasing by inserting words like *some, might, seems, possible* and *hunches* into both paraphrases and questions. These terms, like the use of plurals, widen the potential range of response and reduce the need for surety. Words like *could* and *why* tend to decrease the confidence of listeners and may seem to seek premature commitment to ideas or actions.

Some examples of exploratory language include:

> *"So, you're noticing that **some** of your students are having difficulty with that concept."*

> *"How **might** you go about doing that?"*

> *"You're naming **some possible** solutions. Which **seem** most promising at this point?"*

> *"What are **some** of your **hunches** about why that **may** be so?"*

Syntactical Substitutions
- the---some
- could---might
- is---seems
- why---what

• POSITIVE PRESUPPOSITIONS

Presuppositions are embedded in our language, not in the words, necessarily, but in the assumptions underlying the communication (Elgin, 2000). A positive presupposition communicates our belief in a colleague's capacity and willingness to engage.

For example, we might offer a paraphrase for *"My students just can't do this work"* with *"So, you're concerned about your students' success."* Or, instead of asking, *"Can you see any . . . ?"*, you might say *"As you examine this student's work, what are some of the details that you are noticing?"* or *"As you develop the plan for this class, what are some things that are important to you?"*

Try This
Embedding Positive Presuppositions When Paraphrasing

Construct a paraphrase to respond to each of the following statements. Check your language for its invitational quality. Be particularly aware of positive presuppositions.

1. I don't understand why these kids don't do their homework.

2. My principal visits my classroom every day and I'm worried about what she's thinking.

3. This curriculum is confusing for my students.

4. Parents only contact me when they have a complaint or concern.

Embedding Positive Presuppositions When Asking Questions

Identify the presupposition(s) in each of the following questions. Consider the intention of the question, and rewrite a question that communicates positive presupposition.

1. Do you have any hands-on materials for this lesson?

2. Can you think of any reasons for that behavior?

3. What two things would you change about this assignment?

4. At what point did you notice the lesson wasn't working?

Entering the Protégé's World: Using Paraphrase

The purposeful use of paraphrase signals our full attention. It communicates that we understand the protégé's thoughts, concerns, questions and ideas; or that we are trying to. By signaling that we are listening, we earn permission to inquire for details and press for elaboration. Without the paraphrase, such inquiries can be perceived as interrogation. Well-crafted paraphrases align the speaker and responder, establishing understanding and communicating regard. Questions, no matter how well-intended, distance by degrees the asker from the asked.

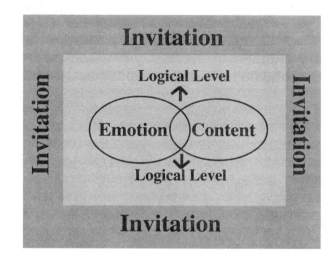

Well-crafted paraphrases with appropriate pauses trigger more thoughtful responses than questions alone. Mediational paraphrasing is a process, driven by:

- Intention to support thinking and problem-solving

- Attention of the paraphraser, who listens fully for the essence of the message

- Communication skills of the paraphraser

In addition to their invitational qualities, mediational paraphrases contain three important elements; they label the speaker's *content*, the speaker's *emotions* about the content and frame a *logical level* for holding the content. Skilled paraphrasing treats responses as gifts. The paraphrase reflects a speaker's thinking back to the speaker for further consideration. It connects the speaker and the listener in a flow of discourse.

Three Types of Paraphrase, Three Intentions

Three types of paraphrase, with three different intentions, widen the range of possible responses for learning-focused mentors. While each supports relationship and thinking, the paraphrase that shifts the level of abstraction of the speaker's language is most likely to create new levels of understanding. While paraphrases often move through a pattern of acknowledging, then summarizing, then shifting level of abstraction, there is no 'right' sequence for application of these responses. Cues from the speaker will help suggest an appropriate response. Versatility in use of paraphrase gives a skillful mentor a wide range of action from which to choose and a more effective repertoire for supporting growth.

• ACKNOWLEDGING AND CLARIFYING
By restating the essence of someone's statements, acknowledging and clarifying paraphrases provide an opportunity to identify and calibrate

content and emotions. By design, they communicate our desire to understand, and our value for the person and what he or she is feeling and saying. Notice the intentional elimination of the personal pronoun 'I' in the paraphrase examples that follow.

For example, a colleague might say:

"I don't know how I'll get all of this work done. I've got a final exam to correct, end-of-term grades and then the paperwork for closing the year!"

To which a mentor might respond:

"You're feeling overwhelmed by all you have to do at this time of the year."

• SUMMARIZING AND ORGANIZING

Summarizing and organizing paraphrases offer themes and containers which shape the initiating statement or separate jumbled issues. This type of paraphrase is useful when there's been a great deal said in a long stream of language.

This type of paraphrase captures the key elements and offers some organization to which the speaker can react. It offers a 'shape' to the initiating statement.

For example, a colleague might say:

"I'm so confused. During language arts, my students work well in groups, participate in class and complete their assignments. In science, they are constantly off-task and I need to keep them doing individual work to keep control in the classroom."

To which a mentor might respond:

"You're noticing significant differences between your students' performance in language arts and their performance in science."

• SHIFTING LEVEL OF ABSTRACTION

Shifting the level of abstraction is a paraphrase that moves language, and therefore, thinking to a higher or lower logical level. The intention of this paraphrase is to illuminate large ideas or categories, often leading the speaker to new discoveries. Or, when shifting down, this paraphrase focuses and clarifies, increasing precision of thinking.

For individuals who think in highly global patterns, the shift down is a way of grounding their thinking in specific examples and details. For individuals who think in highly sequential and concrete patterns, the shift up is a way of helping them explore a bigger picture and provides a wider context for their thoughts.

A Scaffold for Crafting Paraphrases

ACKNOWLEDGE AND CLARIFY

- So, you're feeling _____
- You're noticing that _____
- In other words _____
- Hmm, you're suggesting that _____

SUMMARIZE AND ORGANIZE

- So, there seem to be two key issues here _____ and _____
- On the one hand, there is _____ and on the other hand, there is _____
- For you then, several themes are emerging; _____
- It seems you're considering a sequence or hierarchy here; _____

SHIFTING LEVEL OF ABSTRACTION (UP OR DOWN)

- So, a(n) _____ for you might be _____

(Shifting up)	(Shifting down)
• category	• example
• value	• non-example
• belief	• strategy
• assumption	• choice
• goal	• action
• intention	• option

We move to higher logical levels by naming the big ideas; including concepts, categories, goals and values.

We focus by moving to lower logical levels when abstractions and concepts need grounding in details. We might offer specific details or an example.

For example, a colleague might say:

> *"My kids have trouble getting started, and they're always asking for help."*

To which a mentor might respond:

> *"So, one of your goals is to create greater self-reliance in your learners." (Shift Up)*

Or:

> *"You're finding that your students' are not able to follow directions." (Shift Down)*

A paraphrase that shifts to a higher level of abstraction is often particularly effective in problem-solving situations. Initially, more abstract language widens the potential solution set and encourages broader exploration of ideas and strategies for problem-solving.

For example, a colleague might say:

> *"This math text is much too difficult for many of my students."*

A mentor might paraphrase with:

> *"So, you're looking for instructional materials that meet the needs of all of your students."*

This shift up paraphrase of math text to instructional materials opens the conversation to consider a wider range of solutions to this teacher's concern.

Try This

Paraphrasing works in concert with questioning and pausing to establish and support an environment for thinking. Review the following example. Then try the following exercise to stretch your paraphrasing skills.

Presenting Statement

"I'm really having a hard time with this class. Their ability levels are all over the place and I practically have to plan for 24 different lessons."

ACKNOWLEDGE / CLARIFY	SUMMARIZE / ORGANIZE	SHIFT LEVEL OF ABSTRACTION
"You're concerned about planning for such a diverse group of students."	"So, there seem to be two issues here—the wide range of performance levels in this class; and the need to plan for each student's needs."	"You seem to value providing the appropriate level of learning for each child."

Practice Sample

Craft a paraphrase of each type in response to the following presenting statement.

"I don't see how I can prepare all of my kids to meet the new state standards. They have poor skills and poor attitudes. And we're expected to teach them academic and social skills!"

ACKNOWLEDGE / CLARIFY	SUMMARIZE / ORGANIZE	SHIFT LEVEL OF ABSTRACTION

Designing Questions to Promote Thinking

Skillful mentors are purposeful in their use of questions. A mentor's linquistic repertoire includes the capacity to frame language that opens thinking, as well as language that focuses thinking. Both types of questions mediate thinking. These two categories of mediational questions, inquiring and probing, are an important part of a mentor's toolkit. Inquiries, or questions intended to open thinking, invite multiple responses and are generally asked from a collaborative or coaching stance. These questions communicate a spirit of curiosity and a desire to explore information and ideas. Questions intended to focus thinking probe for increased specificity of information. These questions elicit examples, criteria, and details that support precision in verbal responses. This precision of language reflects precision in thinking. Both types of questions are an important part of the learning-focused mentor's repertoire. Both types of questions contain verbal and nonverbal elements designed to invite thinking.

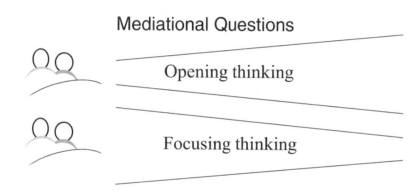

Mediational Questions

Opening thinking

Focusing thinking

Opening Thinking: A Template for Inquiry

Questions that extend and illuminate thinking invite a wide range of potential responses. Language and thinking once surfaced can always be honed and refined. But without it emerging, there is little with which to work. The intention of inquiry is to support a colleague in exploring issues, problems, concerns and ideas.

Similar to the paraphrase, well-crafted inquiries integrate three essential elements; an *invitation* to engage and think, a *topic* to think about and a *cognitive* focus for thinking about the topic.

These elements can be combined in a variety of ways and do not always appear in the same order. Both personal style and context play a part in question construction.

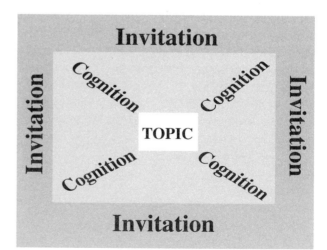

Extending the Invitation: Nondichotomous Questions

Just as with the paraphrase, mediational questions are enveloped by an invitation to think. They, too, require an approachable voice, the use of plurals, attention to exploratory language and communication of positive presupposition. In addition, questions that invite thinking are framed with open-ended, nondichotomous question forms. A nondichotomous question is one which cannot be answered yes or no. For example, instead of asking "Did you notice any unusual behaviors?", ask "What are some of the behaviors you noticed?" In fact, by eliminating dichotomous stems such as "Can you," "Did you," "Will you," or "Have you" we invite thinking and communicate positive presupposition.

Intention-Driven Questions: Providing Cognitive Focus

Planning, problem-solving and reflecting require specific ways of thinking. Learning-focused mentors craft mediational questions that are purposefully driven by a specific cognitive intention. For example, we develop expertise in planning by identifying, predicting and sequencing. Similarly, we make sense of experience by inferring, comparing and analyzing cause and effect. Productive reflection derives from generalizing, hypothesizing, applying and synthesizing. Mediational questions that invite and focus thinking build professional capacity and self-directed learning. Each phase of the Conversation Templates is intended to focus and produce specific cognitive processes. The sidebar on this page offers a sampling of the cognitive processes related to each phase of the Conversation Templates.

Questions that Focus: Probing for Specificity

Vague Language

Our brains filter incoming information, searching for recognizable patterns. From these, we form generalizations that shape and guide thinking. Human language reflects these thinking habits, offering surface vagueness that often masks the rich details that lie beneath. Our brains create and are created by models of reality built from our experiences in the world and from our interpretations of those experiences. We delete and distort incoming and outgoing data to fit these deeply embedded templates (Bandler & Grinder, 1971). As human beings and human brains evolved, generalizations, deletions and distortions in thinking and in language served our hunting and gathering ancestors well, as they made the quick decisions necessary for survival.

These same thinking and language attributes are often barriers in contemporary human communication. One important way that mentors make a difference for novice teachers is by supporting precision in language, which in turn supports precision in thinking. By focusing on and clarifying specifics, the alert mentor can help shift a situation from

Invitational Questions

- Attending Fully
- Approachable Voice
- Plural Forms
- Exploratory Language
- Nondichotomous Forms
- Positive Presupposition

Activating
Recall, estimate, speculate, visualize, count, notice, list, describe, select, observe, predict, forecast

Exploring
Sort, relate, reason, explain, infer, contrast, compare, distinguish, analyze, weigh

Integrating
Evaluate, classify, reflect, summarize, interpret, generalize, deduce, suppose, induce, postulate, hypothesize, theorize, conclude, prioritize

one that might feel overwhelming to the novice, to one that is more manageable emotionally, physically and intellectually. Like many mentoring skills, probing for specificity is based on listening. In this case, listening for vague language and then deciding which terms, if clarified, would support the most productive shifts in thinking.

Vague thinking and language patterns appear within five major categories. These categories become listening lenses for the attuned mentor who selects a focus for clarification, paraphrases the essential ideas, then probes for specificity within target areas. In many cases, more than one category of vagueness appears in the same statement. In all cases, the pattern of pause, paraphrase and then probe is applied.

• Vague Nouns and Pronouns

Vague nouns and pronouns occur commonly in everyday language. In schools we hear about, 'my students', 'the class', 'my fourth period', 'classroom management', 'student behavior', 'technology', 'the parents', 'the administration', 'central office' and a host of other unspecified nouns. For many teachers, someone named 'they' causes most of the problems in their class or school. 'We', 'us', and 'them' are other possible sources of concern and/or joy.

If we hear a protégé say, "my students don't understand fractions," we need to find out how many students are confused about fractions and what elements of fraction learning are most problematic to them. Without these essential details, we can't know where to target our energy and attention within the problem-solving process. Narrowing the field of focus in this case might identify subsets of students with distinct learning needs that can be addressed systematically by the teacher and the students.

Vague Language
- Nouns and Pronouns
- Verbs
- Comparators
- Rule Words
- Universal Quantifiers

We would also need to determine the protégé's definition of 'understand', which leads us to the next category of vagueness.

• Vague Verbs

Planning, problem-solving and reflecting require specificity for focused action and personal learning. The term 'understand' in the vignette above is a prime example. Once we have determined *who* has the problem, we need to clarify the goal of *understanding*. Just what does this teacher mean by 'understanding'; and how will students display their 'understanding'? With some novice teachers, these specifications may lead us to unpacking their understanding of fractions as well.

Teacher goal setting is a ripe area for probing the action words. Words like; 'plan', 'improve', 'design', 'modify', 'enhance' and 'prepare' are all examples of unspecified verbs that have little meaning without clarification and details.

• COMPARATORS

There are two primary types of vagueness relating to comparators; the criteria for comparison and the source of comparison. When our protégé says, *"Today's lesson was much better,"* two queries would be productive; *"In what ways was it better?"* and/or *"What was it better than?"* Until we discover the speaker's criteria for 'better', we don't know how to proceed with the conversation. Is this 'better' a success to build on or are poorly understood factors at work here that leave this 'better' a mystery? Other vague comparators are words like 'best', 'larger', 'slower', 'more', 'less' and 'least'.

Mentors support novice teachers by helping them to specify their criteria and standards for comparison. This action supports rigor in planning and problem-solving, which leads to targeted action and measurable signs of success. When a novice teacher says *"I want students to get better results on my next quiz,"* a mentor might respond by probing for the qualities that would define better results. For example, does the novice mean a higher class average or some other improvements in student responses?

We also often need to surface the lost comparator. For example, was this lesson better than the best lesson the protégé has taught to date—or better than the worst? Our continued conversation would be quite different, depending upon the response.

• RULE WORDS

We all have a set of rules that guide our ways of perceiving and operating in the world. We are not always conscious of these internal codes but they appear in our language when we say things like, "I have to," "I must," "I can't," and "I should have" or "I shouldn't have." When a mentor hears a protégé use a phrase like those above, it may be appropriate to probe for the rule behind the statement. *"Who says you 'have to?'" "What would happen if you didn't?" "What stops you from doing that?"*

Intonation matters greatly here. The mentor's voice must be carefully modulated and nonthreatening to create a safe environment for exploring the internal rules governing the situation.

• UNIVERSAL QUANTIFIERS

"All the parents of my class are upset about the new report card." "The students always get confused when I give directions." Linguists label words and phrases like 'everyone', 'all', 'no one', 'never' and 'always' as universal quantifiers. They also use the term 'deity voice' as a label for this type of language because these terms are spoken as if the statement possesses a universal truth of which 'everyone' is aware. By clarifying the universal quantifier, a mentor helps her protégé ground the conversation with measurable details and supportable data. When the novice says, *"These kids are never here on time,"* the mentor might respond: *"Never? Has there ever been an instance when most of them were on time?"*

Try This

Review the following examples. Identify the vague language. How might you probe for specificity? In what ways would this tool be useful to a learning-focused mentor?

1. These kids never do their homework!

2. Parents don't care.

3. My students are always wild.

4. I'm not ready.

5. I have to do this.

6. This strategy is better.

Extending Thinking

Extending Thinking

- Giving information
- Framing expectations
- Providing resources

Our own knowledge and resource banks form a rich basis for supporting the thinking and problem-solving of others. Mentors extend the thinking of their protégés as they consult, collaborate and coach, by supplying additional information, framing clear expectations for outcomes and processes, and directing the protégé to essential professional resources. These resources might include other professionals in the building or district, print and audiovisual materials, or technologically-based information such as pertinent websites. Such resources might also come in the form of demonstrations of processes such as modeling question-asking protocols or patterns for calling on students. They may include product samples such as worksheets and/or samples of student work.

Again, timing and attention to the effect of our actions is critical in this process. If the information is given too early in the conversation, the protégé may get the impression that we do not think he or she is capable of independent decision-making. If we wait too long and frustration sets in, we unfairly stress our colleague. Our choice of action must align with our intention to extend thinking and simultaneously support the growing relationship.

Section 5 Facilitating Professional Vision: From Novice to Expert Teaching

N O ONE is born knowing how to teach. Classroom instruction is one of the most complex intellectual and emotional tasks that any professional undertakes in our society; and the journey towards expertise is a lifetime's work. Successful journeys begin with skilled counsel and guidance.

In the opening of this book, we offer three goals for learning-focused relationships, suggesting that thoughtful mentors offer support, create challenge, and facilitate a professional vision for their protégés. Each of these intentions requires a vision—of the growth potential of the protégé, of the relationship with the protégé and of the mentor's skill in sustaining productive learning.

For this learning to be increasingly purposeful, mentors need frameworks and language for describing the complexity of teaching. This complexity falls into two main areas: what professional teachers think about and pay attention to in their classrooms; and how they think about it before, during and after instruction. This knowledge base organizes the expert teacher's planning, problem-solving and decision-making. Mental access to these resources supports effective teaching practice that is goal-driven and targeted to the needs of individual students. These capabilities, brought to conscious attention, then guide the mentor's own teaching, modeling and interactions with protégés.

Developing a Vision of Learning

There are no fast tracks to teaching expertise. The road is long, winding and sometimes painful. Amid the noise and energy of schools and schooling, teaching can be a lonely profession. The early years for most novices are filled with doubts about personal effectiveness, teaching competence, and whether one has the personal learning capacities to master this complex profession.

Learning to teach means continually managing the disequilibrium that new questions and newly recognized quandaries produce. Given their limits of attention and their limits of craft knowledge, beginning teachers often do not know what they do not know. There is a vague awareness of some magic that the confident veteran next door seems to possess. But time and energy do not allow exploration of these seeming mysteries. Day-to-day survival and managing newly forming relationships with students, parents and colleagues consumes most available time.

Mentoring, therefore, means a continual balance of supporting current learning needs for one's protégé, with providing appropriate challenges for growth at opportune moments. It also means acknowledging the sense of loss and lowered confidence that often accompanies new awareness of knowledge and skill gaps. These are territories of constructive mismatch that require emotional sensitivity and scrupulous attention to the protégé's current state and developmental level. The information on adult development and teaching expertise outlined in this section is intended to focus the mentor's attention and frame this learning agenda. School-based curriculum initiatives intersect with this repertoire to promote collegiality and learning communities in the school.

According to Jean Piaget, learning is a process of disturbing current constructs with new experiences and exposure to novel ideas. These discoveries then need to be assimilated and/or accommodated to form new conceptual understandings. Skillful mentors know when and how to gently disturb their protégé's current state of development as they escort them on their journey from novice to expert teaching.

Defining Expertise

Developing expertise in any field involves the acquisition, storage and contextually appropriate application of knowledge and skills. A defining characteristic of experts is the ways in which this knowledge base is mentally structured and internally cross-referenced for productive application in both predictable and novel situations. Experts have both richer conceptual bases and greater case knowledge than do novices. Case knowledge is the treasure trove of practical experiences that experts draw upon to solve routine problems. These are the tricks-of-the trade that make professional practice time and energy efficient.

Expert teachers are able to operate both in the moment and over time with clear outcomes in mind; skillfully managing students, content, equipment, materials, the clock and the calendar. They also apply greater complexity and sophistication in analyzing and understanding instructional problems. For example, while managing student learning, master teachers focus first on defining and representing the dilemmas they encounter in their classrooms. In contrast, beginning teachers go directly to developing solutions without first framing the problem (Swanson, O'Connor, and, Cooney, 1990). This difference in the approach to problem-solving is one reason for the importance of the Think-Aloud protocols that we describe in Section Two, Learning-Focused Interactions. By thinking aloud about a problem when taking the consulting stance, a mentor teacher models how an 'expert' contemplates a situation, thereby widening the conceptual, emotional and moral frame for the novice.

Acquiring Craft Knowledge

Day-to-day classroom work draws upon a reservoir of craft knowledge that teachers acquire through the years as they master the various tasks required by their work. In the 1980's, Donald Schon described this wisdom in his seminal work on reflective practice (Schon 1983; 1987). Schon suggests that experienced professionals rely very little on theoretical or academic knowledge to solve practical problems. They rely instead on an extensive body of context specific craft knowledge that allows them to relate past experiences to current situations.

This knowledge is not always explicit; in fact, it may be so well integrated that it seems intuitive to skilled veterans. This automaticity can often be frustrating to novice teachers who are still struggling with basic classroom moves and routines and see their mentors as gifted masters in touch with the secrets of a teaching universe that is still hidden from them.

To transfer the purposes and processes of automated routines and responses to novices, experienced practitioners must first bring these to their own conscious awareness. This is one of the gifts of the mentor/ protégé relationship. Articulating one's own craft knowledge increases its usefulness and extends the craftsmanship of the user.

Craft knowledge and expertise in teaching take time to acquire. The transition from novice to expert occurs in predictable stages. David Berliner identifies the following five stages in this transition (Calderhead, 1996).

TABLE 5.1 NOVICE TO EXPERT STAGES OF TEACHER DEVELOPMENT

1. NOVICE Seeking rules and recipes to guide actions.

2. ADVANCED BEGINNER Seeking contextual and strategic knowledge and beginning to understand when the rules are appropriate and when they might be broken.

3. COMPETENT Making conscious choices about what to do and how to monitor and modify actions to meet goals.

4. PROFICIENT Operating intuitively with know-how, viewing actions holistically within both short and long term goals.

5. EXPERT Integrating the teacher and the task, operating fluently with automaticity and few surprises, in control of the situation.

• NOVICE TEACHERS
Novice teachers seek the comfort of rules and procedures for guidance. With little repertoire to draw from, they attempt to duplicate the structured lessons in the teacher's manual. This might mean preparing

and implementing a guided reading lesson for a specific story in the precise sequence described in the district's reading text. Initially, there is little variation from the scripted text and scant attention to individual student responses. The novice presents the lesson as written in the manual, following her advanced preparation.

• ADVANCED BEGINNER TEACHERS

Advanced Beginner teachers start to stretch the pattern a bit. They are at the early stages of developing richer knowledge about basic classroom operations, their students and teaching specific subjects like reading. They still might use the reading series as a foundation for lessons, but with a bit more comfort and confidence in basic routines, they add strategies like experiential language charts to expand the lesson structure. They also start to modify the sequence that the publisher suggests, incorporating tips from colleagues as they develop personal preferences in both stories and techniques.

• COMPETENT TEACHERS

Competent teachers are goal oriented across a spectrum of instructional concerns. They have the ability to change course during lessons to better meet the immediate needs of learners. During the planning and teaching of a reading lesson, for example, they consider the needs of specific learners and tailor the lesson to help each student develop literacy skills. Assessment of student progress is ongoing and shapes each day's lesson design. The teacher's manual no longer controls instructional practice.

Expert teachers are able to operate both in-the-moment and over time with clear outcomes in mind; skillfully managing students, content, equipment, materials, the clock and the calendar.

• PROFICIENT TEACHERS

Proficient teachers operate at multiple levels simultaneously. They have goals for the class, goals for each student and goals for themselves. They skillfully organize instruction that has both short-term and long-term coherence. Reading lessons, which extend throughout the day and across the curriculum, are not limited to a special period. Students are flexibly grouped and regrouped as skills develop. There is increased attention and greater sophistication in applying informal and formal reading assessments. These are used to organize special interest reading centers for skills development and in-depth exploration of topics popular with students, such as animals and favorite authors.

• EXPERT TEACHERS

Expert teachers expand personal and professional proficiency in all areas of their teaching. There is an organic flow to the day that extends to the ways students self-manage many classroom routines. Teachers at this stage anticipate potential management and learning bottlenecks and intervene before problems emerge. They are able to fluidly apply a vast technical repertoire of knowledge and skills about learning and learners. While seeing children as unique individuals, their personal catalog of learner types helps them to assemble targeted materials and lessons that smooth learning pathways. This confidence and comfort allows them to establish reading routines that promote independence and students' sense of personal responsibility for learning outcomes. Individual and small group conferences enhance students' abilities to self-assess reading difficulties and make appropriate learning choices.

Transitioning From Novice to Expert

According to Berliner, the novice stage occupies the first year of teaching. Most teachers reach the competence stage after three or four years, with only a modest proportion moving to the proficient stage and fewer still attaining expert status. The growth from novice to more expert teaching requires more than simple experience. It is also a highly personal voyage through the seas of adult development. Having a skilled navigator along to plot the course and find safe harbors increases the safety of the journey and allows one to enjoy the adventure. Skilled mentors come equipped with a chart, a compass, and knowledge of the route ahead.

Expert teachers . . . also apply greater complexity and sophistication in analyzing and understanding instructional problems.

Accompanying and focusing this journey are phases and changes in cognitive, ego and moral development. Awareness of these changes informs the quality and kinds of mentor-protégé interactions. It is important to remember that young teachers fresh out of college are not fully formed adults. They have many developmental challenges to master at the same time that they are mastering a new and demanding profession. Gaps in thinking, fragile egos and moral dilemmas are to be expected and will need to be supported.

Cognitive Development

Developing higher level thinking is a major goal of skillful mentoring. There are numerous studies correlating teachers' conceptual development with improved outcomes for students. Teachers at higher conceptual levels are more able to read and flex in the classroom, continually adapting the learning environment and methods to better meet the needs of individual students (Hunt 1976; 1981). These greater conceptual abilities make expert teaching possible.

To develop such flexibility, mentors encourage and mediate thinking during learning-focused conversations, as outlined in Section Two, Learning-Focused Interaction. The Conversation Templates themselves are organized around specific cognitive processes. These are embedded directly within the questions at each phase of the conversations. The challenge for the mentor is to transcend episodic problem-solving and solution thinking to widen the frame beyond immediate issues. Higher level thinking involves the complex processes of formal operational thinking. (See Table 5.2: Piaget's Levels of Formal Operational Thinking).

TABLE 5.2 PIAGET'S LEVELS OF FORMAL OPERATIONAL THINKING (ADAPTED FROM FLAVELL, 1985)

- **ABSTRACT THINKING** Considering a variety of possibilities.

- **COMBINATORIAL THINKING** Considering all possible combinations of ideas.

- **HYPOTHETICAL THINKING** Considering what-ifs and potential scenarios.

- **PROJECTIVE THINKING** Thinking across multiple time horizons.

- **METACOGNITIVE THINKING** Awareness and self-regulation of one's own thinking processes.

- **REFLECTIVE THINKING** Reflecting upon and learning from actions and experiences.

By intentionally crafting questions designed to focus and exercise complex thinking, and by modeling these processes themselves, learning-focused mentors offer access to increasingly sophisticated conceptual frames.

Adult Development

Studies of teacher development support the notion of stages through which all practitioners pass. King and Kitchener (1994) note that adult growth is slow, with no regressions and no skipping of stages. They also found that age by itself does not predict or promote growth in reflective judgment. Across a variety of adult settings, informal education and professional development experiences were the greatest contributors to growth. For novice teachers, mentors are an important resource for promoting progress in these areas.

Stages of ego and moral reasoning greatly influence the classroom environment that a teacher creates. Higher levels of moral reasoning inspire more democratic classroom practices, including teacher-to-student relationships, student-to-student relationships, discipline practices and overall emotional climate (Chang, 1994).

The various stage theories highlight important aspects of human development and offer a guide for mentors as they manage their relationship with protégés and attempt to balance the intersecting goals of supporting, challenging and facilitating professional vision. This equation computes differently for each protégé depending on present conditions and current stages of cognitive, ego and moral development.

Mentoring Across Developmental Stages

A protégé's developmental stage influences a mentor's decisions regarding the stance to take with a given issue. Given various combinations of a novice's craft knowledge, conceptual, ego and moral development, an attuned mentor balances her approach and navigates across the continuum of interaction; consulting, collaborating and coaching as is most appropriate to support the developmental needs of her protégé. The hardest call is knowing when to stand firm and help a novice struggle through a difficult decision-making process rather than solving the problem for him or her. What is obvious and appropriate to the skilled veteran is often hidden from the novice's view. By appreciating these instances as developmental differences, we are then able to seize the teachable moment and support learning and growth in a meaningful way.

Metacognition as an Organizer for Professional Practice

Experts think differently about their practice than do novices. They also think about their thinking differently. Metacognition refers to two aspects of higher thinking processes. One is awareness of one's thinking processes while they are occurring. The other is the self-regulation of these processes.

A skilled chemistry teacher notices something is not right in her classroom. The noise level and level of student attention to the lab task does not match her sense of what is most appropriate for this lesson. As an expert teacher and expert thinker she first notices her own awareness, remembering how she might have responded in her first years of teaching. She quickly scans the class to gather additional information to formulate her next decision. She controls the impulse to admonish students for their behavior. The wisdom of experience has taught her that when students are off-task, there might be something wrong with the task itself. These thoughts and the monitoring of these thoughts all occur in split seconds as she mentally sorts out possible issues and possible actions.

Moving to the center of the lab, she calls for a pause in the action and calmly asks selected students to describe the source of their confusion. This action restores a sense of order and purposefulness to the room. By noticing and controlling her thinking, this master teacher is able to resolve this issue and smoothly extend student learning. Had she reacted impulsively, without monitoring and controlling her inner responses, she might have broken the lesson flow by contributing to student distraction and breaking momentum for all involved.

Expert teachers exercise metacognitive skills in a variety of ways, monitoring decisions, choices and the impact of actions. This is the inner voice of expertise. As they access this resource, master teachers continually sort through their internalized knowledge-bases about the structure of the discipline they are currently teaching, their instructional repertoire, knowledge of the individual students with whom they are working and knowledge about their own goals, values and beliefs. We describe these knowledge-bases in more detail later in this section. As they sort this treasure-trove of options, master teachers mentally articulate and apply clear criteria for their selections.

It is the kinds and qualities of their filters that most separates experts from novices. Expert teachers are able to pursue multiple goals for a wider variety of students during the flow of the lesson than are novices. They always have big picture outcomes for thinking and social skills and continually reinforce them. They manage relationships with the whole class at the same time that they intervene with and support individual learners. Experts design specific lessons that fit within a bigger curriculum plan that is operating all the time. Beginning teachers tend to be more immediate, intent on managing the flow of a specific lesson plan or controlling student behavior.

Self-regulation of thinking processes is the essence of intention-driven action in the classroom. This vital feedback loop helps alert teachers calibrate their choices and behaviors with their intentions, encouraging in-flight reflection and self-monitoring. This attention might mean monitoring the pace of one's speech and use of pauses to elicit student thinking. It also might mean controlling emotions when responding to a difficult student. In essence, it is the thermostat of self-control that regulates attention, task-focus, impulsiveness, humor and a host of emotional, mental and physical responses.

Opportunities to Develop Complex Thinking Skills

• REFLECTION

Just as technical repertoire and deeper conceptual understandings of the craft of teaching develop over time and are enriched and accelerated by supportive mentoring, so is the skill and disposition for increased metacognition. The Reflecting Template detailed in Section Three, is especially important in this area. Inquiries that support reflection on actions taken and not taken can be enlarged to explore the cues and thinking processes that stimulated the protégé's decisions and behaviors. Such explorations help novices to understand themselves as teachers and to realize the ways in which their patterns of attention and thought create the classroom environment around them. Over time, this awareness leads to increased confidence and a greater sense of efficacy—a belief that they can direct and control positive outcomes for their students (Chester & Beaudin, 1996; Tschannen-Moran, Hoy & Hoy, 1998).

Skilled teachers typically consider three areas as they reflect upon lessons—technical dimensions, practical considerations and critical aspects (Calderhead, 1996). Technical reflection focuses on whether learning objectives for that lesson were met. This reflection is based on specific success criteria. Practical reflection focuses on the appropriateness and effectiveness of particular strategies and the outcomes of those actions. Critical reflection focuses on the deeper purposes of lessons, learning and learning processes.

By reflecting with the protégé after lessons have been taught, mentors support the re-examination of earlier thinking and help novices make connections as they analyze successes and review shortcomings.

Expert teachers exercise metacognitive skills in a variety of ways, monitoring decisions, choices and the impact of actions. This is the inner voice of expertise.

• PLANNING

In addition, lesson planning is an important opportunity for mentors to support the development of a novice's thinking capacities (Clark and Peterson, 1986). By encouraging detailed planning that explores choice points and monitoring strategies, mentors help novices develop the habits of mind of more skilled practitioners. By observing and participating in a protégé's planning, mentors gain insight into mental processes and can develop tailored strategies to support and extend thinking in this area.

By noting where in the planning process a novice needs the most support, a skilled mentor can decide when and how to move from coaching to consulting during a given conversation. She can also note general patterns of thought for this protégé and know when to support, and when and how to challenge this individual.

• CLASSROOM OBSERVATION

Classroom observation is another useful arena for gathering information about the protégé's thinking processes. Detailed observations about choice points, transitions, lesson structure and student responses can all be used to frame inquiries into the novice's immediate focus and what he or she needs to anticipate in future lesson plans.

An Expert Teacher's Professional Lenses

The knowledge base on teaching is both wide and deep (Saphier and Gower, 1997). For our purposes, we are organizing it here within four broad regions. We examine knowledge of the structure of the discipline(s); self; teaching skills and strategies; and learners and learning.

These lenses provide frameworks for exploring growth areas for novice teachers. They provide organizers for the mentor to structure learning-focused conversations with a protégé; to set learning goals; and to assemble resources for supporting and sustaining growth in personal and craft knowledge. These lenses are also useful to a mentor for her own teaching and work with other colleagues.

Knowledge of the Structure of the Discipline

Teacher knowledge of the structure of a given content discipline correlates highly with student success in that area. This understanding moves beyond content knowledge alone and into the organization of knowledge within each domain. The structure of the discipline means knowing the big ideas within a content area; the organizing principles, key concepts and the ways in which they influence one another (Shulman, 1987). In elementary mathematics, for example, understanding means being able to explain and illustrate a sense of

TABLE 5.3 DEVELOPING PROFESSIONAL CAPACITIES

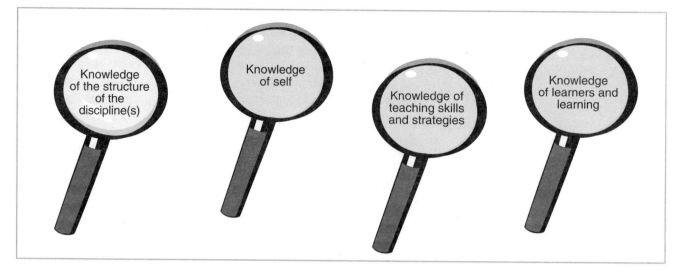

number and how various operations such as addition and subtraction relate to each other. In social studies, it means showing students how to apply geographic, political, historical, economic and social perspectives to a given situation.

These deeper understandings greatly influence lesson design and lesson flexibility so that students can develop meaningful cognitive maps of their own (Darling-Hammond, 1997). When teachers have fragmented understandings themselves, they transfer these to their students and contribute to student misconceptions within that content area.

Teachers with rich structural knowledge are more flexible and resourceful in meeting the challenges that arise during classroom lessons. Real learning is messy. Students do not always fit neatly within the boundaries of lesson plans. Therefore, teacher content knowledge must always be greater and more complexly structured than that of their students. This allows teachers to prioritize and select those content objectives most appropriate for their students.

During planning and reflecting conversations, mentors need to listen carefully for gaps in a novice teacher's understanding of important curricular ideas. Creating a climate in which it is safe for a protégé to ask for help with content understandings is a necessary condition for growth. No one, least of all a beginning teacher, knows everything about a discipline. This is especially true for elementary teachers and others who teach more than one content area. Providing resource materials and including mini-tutorials during conversations reduces the novice's anxiety and at the same time helps to ensure content accuracy for that teacher's students.

It is important for teachers to understand and be able to model the specialized ways of thinking in a given field. Literature and physical science, for example, each have their own principles of inquiry. In social studies, ideas are organized in specific ways. Mathematics has a rich problem-solving repertoire. Writing narrative text is different than writing expository text. Each of these ways of knowing is a rich element within its content area. By promoting these skills and perspectives, teachers help students discover how those who produce knowledge and knowing in a specific domain develop and modify ideas. So, too, mentors create these understandings for their protégés.

Each content area is a minefield of misconceptions. Experienced teachers learn to anticipate these as they appear within curriculum topics. Their lesson plans reflect this thinking as they design ways to surface and dispel these barriers to deeper understanding. Knowing which misconceptions are developmentally appropriate at certain stages of learning is valuable craft knowledge. Knowing how to help students work through them is even more useful. The blend of content knowledge, learner knowledge and teaching knowledge that connects subject matter to targeted learning strategies is called pedagogical content knowledge (Shulman, 1987). Expert teachers assemble and draw upon a rich collection of analogies, models, memory aids and explanatory approaches to represent ideas and understandings to their students. They also develop tricks-of-the-trade for helping students to grapple willingly with misconceptions and to accept these as part of the learning process. Helping a protégé anticipate likely misconceptions and sharing instructional solutions is one way that mentors welcome novices to the joys of teaching and learning in a given content area.

For mentors it is important to remember that individual teachers approach each subject differently (Shulman, 1987). For elementary teachers this means the ways they approach specific content areas such as reading or mathematics. For secondary teachers this usually means specific topics within a curriculum.

One study of first year biology teachers noted that when the novices were presenting topics with which they had great depth of knowledge, they let their classes explore ideas as they asked questions that were more open-ended and promoted richer classroom discourse. When the novices were less confident of their own content knowledge, lessons were structured more rigidly the teachers themselves talked more and asked lower cognitive level questions (Carlson, 1991).

A novice's approach to specific subject areas is a special consideration for mentors of both elementary and secondary teachers. The choice of stance—consulting, collaborating or coaching may need to be weighted differently for different content areas or curriculum topics. While beginning teachers encounter a general set of universal challenges, content specific issues need to be analyzed for possible interventions. If classroom management issues crop up at specific times of day, the protégé's comfort with a specific subject area maybe a factor to consider.

A mentor's own content knowledge is a factor here as well. We all have our stretch areas. Sharing these with a protégé communicates a belief in lifelong learning. It is possible that the protégé may have content strengths to share with the mentor and can contribute to mutual learning in that manner.

Knowledge of Self

Knowledge of self includes the territories of conceptual, ego and moral development mentioned earlier in this section. It also includes knowledge of the personal values, beliefs and standards that guide daily decision-making. If teachers are to be effective with an increasingly diverse student population, they need to recognize and understand their own worldviews before they can appreciate and honor the worldviews of their students (McAllister & Irvine, 2000).

Values and beliefs shape the perceptions and judgments that carry teachers through their days. They undergird the goals teachers set for themselves and for their students. Beliefs and values are the most influential element in the type of classroom culture and learning environment that teachers develop with their students (Pajares, 1992).

Beliefs about the nature of learning and the purposes and process of teaching shape curricular and instructional preferences. These beliefs also shape personal standards for what students should learn and the desired qualities of student performances and products. In what ways is learning about the transmission of important cultural knowledge and the development of basic skills? In what ways is it about developing students' thinking and problem-solving skills and capacities? In what ways is it about developing a just society infused with democratic principles? In what ways is it about helping students discover and reach for their full potentials as human beings? And in what ways is it about promoting students' ethical and spiritual development (Eisner, 1994)?

These goals often overlap. In the heat of teaching and with the press of the clock and calendar, each teacher makes decisions about what to emphasize and what to let slide. These choices are at heart a matter of values and beliefs. Bringing these to conscious attention helps a protégé navigate conflicting options and the sometimes conflicting goals he or she encounters when his or her own beliefs bump headlong into institutional beliefs and values. Current stages of adult development influence how each teacher resolves these dilemmas. Caring mentors support these explorations as vital lessons on the road to developing confidence and expertise as a teacher.

Knowledge of one's own learning style preferences is a special area of self-knowledge. It is important for novice teachers to realize that their preferred style may not be that of all of their students. Some of us perceive and process the world globally. Others prefer more sequential approaches. Some of us are task-driven and others are relationship driven. Some of us are visually dominant and others orient towards kinesthetic or auditory processing strategies (Guild & Garger, 1998).

All these style preferences, and the many subtle ways they manifest themselves, appear in our teaching. The ability to stretch against one's own preferred style is the hallmark of flexibility and the mark of a master teacher who can connect with a wide variety of learners.

Style is also an important area for mentors to consider in their interactions with protégés. Flexibility in approach is especially important when the mentor and the protégé have very different learning style preferences. The mentor needs to remember that these are preferences and that the most resourceful people can stretch and flex as needed. It is also useful to remember that under stress we revert to our most dominant learning styles. This means that mentors need to be especially aware of this dimension during times of predictable stress as noted in the phases of first year teaching we describe in Section One, The Mentor's Role. It is also an important consideration when a protégé has had a particularly trying experience and needs to process it.

We all have our stretch areas. Sharing these with a protégé communicates a belief in lifelong learning.

The reflecting conversation, detailed in Section Three, Maximizing Time and Attention, offers an opportunity for sorting out the dilemmas and tensions novices encounter in their daily work. Blocks or confusions in thinking are often a sign that the protégé has encountered a situation with students, parents or colleagues that violates some deeply held value or belief. This belief may not have consciously surfaced yet, but it is at the heart of this particular matter. A skilled mentor will focus the conversation by exploring tensions from the protégé's point of view to help him or her discover the values that he or she perceives are being violated. With self-knowledge as a frame, the mentor and protégé can then pursue other perspectives and possible approaches to the situation. The mentor may also need to take a consulting stance to share other viewpoints and alternative explanations that have not occurred to the protégé.

Knowledge of Teaching Skills and Strategies

Expert teachers, like concert violinists, consciously develop their performance repertoires. They assemble and hone micro routines that are combined and applied to fit a wide variety of conditions and settings. Master teachers automatize many routines and basic moves to free cognitive space for more sophisticated sensing of the needs of their learners. Such unconscious competence is the mark of an expert in the classroom. The lack of automaticity with basic moves, such as getting and maintaining student attention, giving clear directions and establishing routines for smooth classroom transitions, consumes the emotional and physical energy of beginning teachers. This is why these and other areas of basic classroom management are usually the first level of concerns addressed in the mentor-protégé relationship. Until these fundamentals are under control, there is often little space for more sophisticated investigations of instructional practice.

Lack of comfort in these arenas blocks protégé's openness to ideas and resources that address other areas of teaching practice. It is often useful to front load face-to-face time at the beginning of the school year to share practical strategies and routines that work well in the mentor's own classroom. This is a prime area for initial Idea Banks or to supply a 'tip-of-the-week.'

Content specific pedagogy is an important variable that increases student success (Wenglinsky, 2000). Students whose teachers help them to develop higher-order thinking and problem-solving skills linked to specific content areas outperform students whose teachers only convey lower-order skills (McLaughlin & Talbert, 1993). Mentors support this essential part of the novice to expert journey when they conduct model lessons for novices that emphasize these aspects of teaching. They also extend the protégé's skills during planning activities when they inquire into these elements. This is a place where the consulting stance adds great value at the point in the conversation when specific teaching techniques are being considered.

Knowledge of Learners and Learning

Knowledge of who learners are and how each learns best guides the special relationship between teacher and students. The greatest teaching repertoire in the world is wasted if it is not well matched to the needs of learners (Saphier & Gower, 1997). The push for smaller class sizes and smaller schools is a response to the need to know one another. In an increasingly diverse world, personal knowledge and close relationships help to connect learners to teachers, to important ideas and to each other.

The exploding knowledge base about brain development, learning styles, multiple intelligence, developmental differences and cultural patterns energizes Lee Shulman's conception of the need for pedagogical learner knowledge on the part of all teachers (Shulman, 1987). Developmental differences extend far beyond the primary grades. Over the years, these differences amplify as the span between students widens in Piagetian terms. There are many middle school and high school students who operate at a solid concrete operational level. These learners often run headlong into a curriculum organized by abstractions introduced through symbol systems. When teachers recognize these learning patterns and

In an increasingly diverse world, personal knowledge and close relationships help to connect learners to teachers, to important ideas and to each other.

they approach instruction flexibly, they begin lessons and units with concrete experiences, then help students represent ideas with pictures and graphics as they support student language development and meaning making. This pathway leads students to firmer conceptual development and richer understandings of abstract ideas (Lipton & Wellman, 2000).

Given a changing student population, there is an increasing need for culturally respectful approaches to teaching and learning. Materials and methods that engage one population of learners may confuse or offend another. There is an important overlap here for teachers between this area and knowledge of self. How a teacher came to know an idea or discipline may not be an appropriate or effective cultural match for the students to which he or she is now teaching that same material. Mentors support novices by providing teaching tips in this arena. In fact, attending to and celebrating cultural diversity is a good area for which to develop Idea Banks.

Language differences are emerging as an important variable for teachers to consider. There is a critical variance between students' social discourse and their formal knowledge of the structure and norms of academic discourse in specific content fields (Lee & Fradd, 1998). Skilled teachers help students bridge their own language to formal academic language, integrating personal and cultural relevance with content understandings. This learning is more robust and more likely to be retained by students. This concept means that ultimately all teachers, no matter what their content specialties, are teachers of language and teachers of thinking.

Mentoring as a Professional Vision

To mentor is to teach.

To teach is to learn.

As mentors gain experience and perspective on the craft of mentoring, they gain new insights into themselves as teachers and as learners. This learning occurs on multiple levels. On one level, mentors develop richer understandings about the craft of teaching. While engaging in personal reflection and articulating their own knowledge base to novices, they deepen and integrate personal knowledge about professional practice. On another level, mentors revisit their own history as teachers as they monitor the growth of their protégés and come to see the parallel between this journey and the journey all learners take in any new field of endeavor. Yet on another level, the mentor is learning about the art of supporting novice teachers. This, too, becomes a voyage of discovery in the passage from novice to expert mentoring.

Section 6　Strategies for Success

THE strategies shared in the following pages are practical extensions and enhancements of the mentoring relationship. As these tips and tricks require varying investments of time and resources, they are organized by degree of effort required for implementation. They range from minimal time and energy to moderate investments to more extensive commitments. Additionally, these useful strategies are organized by most appropriate time of year for application. Some ideas are great for the beginning or end of the school year, while others may be ongoing. You may want to correlate these ideas with the Calendar of Options in Section One, The Mentor's Role.

Beginning of Year   Minimal Investment

Meet, Greet and Share

Purpose: To connect protégés with the faculty in a way that addresses both personal and professional needs.

Schedule a brief meeting before or after school for grade level/content area personnel. Ask each attendee to bring two things to the meeting: a funny classroom memory and a favorite teaching resource. While sharing snacks and beverages, take the opportunity to share favorite resources as well as memorable experiences. This exchange provides the protégé with additional resource ideas, reinforces a collegial school culture and attends to affective needs as well.

Extensions

Capture resources and stories in a journal for future reference and sharing.

Each member prepares an index card describing "What I know now that I wish I had known then."

Use the Meet, Greet and Share for a mentor and/or protégé support group meeting.

Tips

Include protégés in sharing memories and resources from pre-service experiences.

Pace the meeting to ensure appropriate time for discussion of resources including how and when they have been used, practical tips for use and where and how to locate them.

Welcome To . . . Basket

Purpose: To provide the protégé with items that are useful but may be forgotten in routine preparations. To establish connections between the protégé and existing faculty.

Construct a Welcome To (school name) Basket filled with useful personal and professional items. Invite colleagues to provide items for the basket as appropriate. Suggested items include:

Post-it notes

Pens

Dots or pointers for use with the overhead projector

A coupon book with free services such as one lunch duty, assistance with paperwork, etc.

Throat lozenges

Tissues

Instructional books or journals

Snacks

A box of colored chalk

Item with school insignia, such as a school poster, T-shirt or coffee mug

Extensions

As a faculty, construct a list of 'Top Ten Things' you need or need to know and include in all Welcome To . . . Baskets. This interaction also serves as an interactive, collegial activity for staff.

With colleagues, design a 'Red Letter Dates' calendar to include in the baskets. In addition to traditional dates, these calendars might indicate vacations, staff social events, cultural events in the community, theater offerings too good to miss and other renewal activities.

Design different baskets for veteran teacher protégés concentrating more on their specific needs in the new assignment.

Tip

Keep the contents of the basket light and somewhat fanciful as a break from what might be an overwhelming amount of instructional and logistical information at the beginning of the year.

Beginning of Year   Minimal Investment

New Teacher Luncheon/Shower

Purpose: To acquaint new staff with existing staff and community resources. This event promotes collegiality and allows for personal and professional relationship building.

Plan a luncheon or shower for all new teachers. This group should include novices and veterans new to the school (or district), as well as staff transferred from within the system. For a luncheon, plan a covered dish or a box lunch. A shower might be held after school with snacks.

Include in the luncheon or shower 'goodie bags' or gift boxes that might contain items such as:

Coupon book where you have assembled discounts for local businesses, free soft drink or other snacks.

Copy of the previous year's annual or yearbook to be used to match faces with names.

School insignia items such as T-shirt, coffee mugs or canvas bags.

Map of the school with a listing of personnel and assignments including specialized support and committees.

Highlighted and annotated handbook of policies, procedures and regulations.

Items for the classroom such as bulletin board border, timer, patterns or templates for instructional materials and pens/pencils.

Extensions

Invite parents, members of the community and business representatives.

Include maps of the local area and locations of other schools in the gifts and goodies.

Invite staff to each bring a grab bag with a concealed item to be swapped with other staff so each person leaves with something.

Tips

Coordinate the event to ensure that each staff person leaves with a goodie.

Organize activities during the luncheon/shower that serve as getting-to-know you or, for existing staff, getting-to-know you better energizers.

Plan for opportunities to highlight parents, business and community members that are present. Provide time for sharing and exchanging information and resources with them.

Joint Planning Session

Purpose: To collaboratively plan for the first week of school.

Ideally, this session is held at least two weeks prior to the beginning of the school year. Additional planning sessions may be held at the beginning of the second semester or at any point when a need or desire arises for collaborative planning. The Planning Template may be used to structure conversations regarding lessons or segments of instruction (see Section Three, Maximizing Time and Attention).

Schedule a minimum of 60 minutes of uninterrupted time.

Jointly discuss and plan for the first day of school.

Collaboratively plan for physical arrangement of the room, instructional displays, use of funds that may be provided by the district for materials, etc.

Review curriculum requirements.

Explore instructional plans for the first week of school.

Extensions

Use the Joint Planning Session to establish professional and personal goals as well as student goals.

Open the Planning Session to include grade level/content area staff.

If possible, conduct separate planning sessions for management issues and instructional issues.

Tips

Allot portions of time during the session to share information perceived as critical for beginning the year and to surface questions/concerns of the protégé.

Be attentive to balancing information with time for processing and application.

Schedule subsequent sessions for addressing questions that will emerge from the implementation of plans.

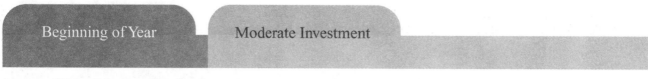

Incredible Ideas Scrapbook

Purpose: To efficiently provide protégés with classroom-tested ideas and resources.

The Scrapbook may be assembled prior to the beginning of the school year and supplemented at the beginning of the second semester as the mentor continues to collect strategies. Ask colleagues to submit donations to the scrapbook as well. Possibilities to include are:

Teaching stories

Poems

Cartoons

Get acquainted ideas/icebreakers

Tips for remembering student names

Favorite fillers

Index cards with strategies for grouping students, learning-center activities, etc.

Bulletin board display ideas

Extensions

Extend the scrapbook to include instructional ideas, assessment strategies and website references.

Categorize the ideas by content area, time of year, state standard, etc.

Develop the scrapbook as a grade level or content area collaborative project.

Create a book of archetypes illustrating state or district standards.

Ask the protégé to add to the ideas and share with others.

Tips

Ideas and suggestions should include type of application, time required, do's and don'ts for successful implementation.

Identify the contributor of each idea to allow for follow-up questions.

Extensive Investment | Beginning of the Year

Professional Portfolios

Purpose: To establish clear expectations and connect the mentoring relationship to high professional standards.

Using the National Teaching Standards for Beginning Teachers (see Section Seven, Appendix), or state or district standards for excellence, conduct a goal setting conversation which is concrete, specific and lays out plans for achieving goals, as well as evidence that will support the protégé's self-assessment.

Apply the Planning Template to this interaction, and keep a record of the goals as reference for future conversations.

Begin a portfolio as an ongoing source of self-assessment and reference for continued conversations (see Section Seven, Appendix).

Portfolio items might include:

Sample lesson plans
Samples of student work
Pictures of bulletin board displays or learning centers
Items and artifacts created for classroom lessons
Letters and comments from parents
Reflections and anecdotes from the protégé's journal

Extensions

Encourage your protégé to keep a reflective journal (see Section Eight, Structured Forms, Tools and Blacklines). As the portfolio is developed, select pages might be included.

Collaborate with your protégé by keeping a Double-Entry Journal. Your protégé enters thoughts, ideas, concerns and questions in the left hand column (or on the left page of the book) and leaves it for you. You enter responses on the opposite side.

Keep a professional portfolio of your own, and share entries and insights.

Tips

Create an organizing scheme for the portfolio, and limit the number of items to 4-6 a month.

Be sure the items in the portfolio relate to the goals established at the beginning of the year. Review the portfolio as a method for reflecting on these goals.

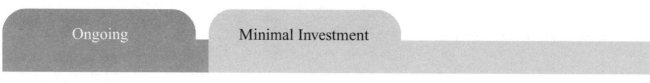

Got It/Need It

Purpose: To efficiently manage resources and provide optimal access to sometimes limited materials or equipment.

Post a chart or worksheet in the library, staff room or Professional Nook (see page 90).

Ask staff members to record items they are willing to share in the Got It column and items needed in the Need It column.

Date	Got It	Need It	Date

Extensions

Post this information at staff meetings and provide a brief period of time to update.

Place this information online to encourage sharing among schools.

Tips

Include items purchased by the school or found in the library on the chart to increase communication about resources among staff.

Identify a 'point person' to keep the chart updated.

Use the most requested items, or most used items, as data for future purchasing decisions.

Lively Lifelines

Purpose: To capitalize on support resources for the protégé. To encourage networking.

Assist the protégé in networking with other professionals by:

Locating someone to serve as a 'phone-a-friend' resource when a question that must be answered immediately arises.

Soliciting volunteers to participate as e-mail partners to provide information, forward pertinent correspondence, etc.

Identifying a 'go-to' mentor that may be in close proximity to the protégé's classroom and may serve as a substitute mentor as needed.

Introducing the protégé to other professionals and assisting with networking.

Acquainting the protégé with the teacher center and other district-based resources.

Extensions

Include agencies and professionals in the community in the networking process.

Use technology to network with online resources, including appropriate listservers.

Encourage membership in professional organizations.

Tips

Check with the protégé periodically to ensure communication lines are working.

Include contacts for logistical and clerical assistance, as well as instructional resources.

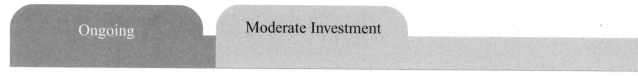

Ongoing   Moderate Investment

Professional Nook

Purpose: To provide a mechanism for sharing up-to-date literature, research, newsletters and other important and interesting information. To provide a conducive space for professional reading.

Establish a comfortable space in the faculty room, school library or other appropriate area for a reading corner. Strategically select the location for minimal traffic and noise if possible. Consider aesthetics by providing lighting, seating and a table to hold items. Possible sources of reading materials include:

Professional reading such as journals or recent books.

Donated graduate school and higher education resources.

Current magazine articles that may have been highlighted by a previous reader.

Display of trade samples.

School newletters.

System memorandums.

Extensions

Ask protégés to donate readings and materials from recent and continuing studies.

Develop Professional Nooks for each grade level, grade clusters or department.

Organize reading materials that focus on a current local initiative.

Arrange for study groups to meet periodically (e.g. once per month) and cluster reading around the study group's topic.

Tips

Refresh these materials often so information does not become stale.

Ask for a volunteer, possibly the library media specialist, to oversee the ongoing project.

Moderate Investment

Ongoing

Problem-Solving Partnership

Purpose: To reinforce norms of collaborative problem-solving.

Both the mentor and protégé will encounter opportunities to share expertise and satisfy mutual or individual needs.

Designate a meeting when each person will bring a presenting problem or issue to the table.

Discuss and surface the desired outcome for one of the presenting problems.

Brainstorm options for reaching the desired outcome (brainstorming encourages creativity by removing judgment).

Mutually discuss criteria for selecting action options.

Repeat this process, as time allows, for each participant.

Extensions

Use Problem-Solving Partnerships at a grade level, department or staff meeting activity. Schedule time at a subsequent meeting to update and discuss progress, additional decisions, questions, etc.

Apply this strategy with students for teaching problem-solving skills.

Include in mentor and/or protégé support group meetings.

Extend problem-solving to 'what happens if' sessions.

Tips

Attend to pacing during the meeting to make sure both partners share.

Begin with the mentor's problem to ease anxiety and model the lifelong learning process.

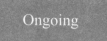

Ongoing | Extensive Investment

Collaborative Role-Alike Support Groups

Purpose: To provide ongoing support for both protégés and mentors and feedback for assessing the mentoring program.

Both mentors and protégés need structured opportunities to collaboratively problem-solve, seek guidance and provide mutual support. Convening each group separately allows for enhanced learning and increased effectiveness in the mentoring relationship. It is also important to be time efficient during the meetings. Suggestions for structuring these include:

Conduct meetings once per quarter.

Include an entry in reflection journals at the beginning of each meeting.

Structure some reflection prompts to surface issues, concerns, successes and constructive suggestions for refining the program.

Provide at least one new idea, strategy or tool that can be implemented immediately (include content regarding educational practice).

Reserve a portion of time (minimum of 15 minutes) for trio problem-solving, allowing each member of the trio to state a presenting problem and request consulting, collaborating or coaching from the remaining members.

Provide written communication updating events, policy changes, logistical information, etc.

Extensions

Design support groups for experienced administrators, beginning administrators and assistants.

Survey participants periodically to determine 'burning issues' for discussion.

Tips

Allow written communication to speak for itself and clarify when needed.

Pace the meetings according to the agenda and participant needs.

Collaborative Staff Development

Purpose: To promote team planning and implementation of content-driven staff development sessions.

Collaborative interactions and reciprocal learning are value-added components of the mentoring relationship. Considering district initiatives and mutual foci for growth, identify a staff development opportunity to attend together. Following the staff development, reflect on the learnings and decide on strategies for implementation. Jointly agree on assessment methods and data collection. Also, use the Planning and Reflecting Templates to guide learning-focused conversations.

Extensions

Jointly assess results from data collections and formulate conclusions.

Share results with grade level, content area and other faculty members.

Pair with a mentor/protégé team at another school to compare strategies, results and successes. This active sharing increases the knowledge base for all.

Plan and implement a special integrated project.

Tips

Remember to include tips, adaptations and important things to remember when sharing results with other professionals.

Use student feedback in refining, revising and reporting on your work.

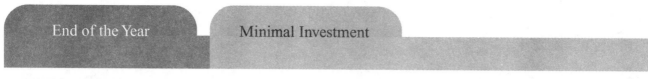

End of the Year   Minimal Investment

Packing Up

Purpose: To provide an opportunity to collectively prepare for the closing of school and an informal opportunity to reflect and debrief on the year's experiences.

The mentor and protégé jointly plan and complete activities to close the school year. The time spent working together may also be used as a time for sharing and wondering in an informal way. The mentoring partnership may complete some or all of these activities for both rooms.

Jointly organize materials and supplies.

Prepare for end-of-year reports such as attendance, inventory and resource allocation.

Discuss and complete student reports such as grades, cumulative records and library records.

As you work, think out loud regarding learnings from this year. Engage in conversations about expectations for next year's assignment.

Extensions

Develop or update checklists to guide end-of-year activities.

Involve grade-level or content area teams in this process.

Tips

Implement as a collaborative activity allowing the protégé the opportunity to be on equal footing as much as possible.

Encourage the protégé to share exciting or interesting ideas and strategies that were particularly successful.

Moderate Investment   End of the Year

Celebrate Success

Purpose: To recognize individual and staff efforts and successes. To share and spread effective ideas. To acknowledge professional and personal efforts.

You may choose to celebrate projects, partnerships, initiative implementations and other noteworthy accomplishments by:

Reminding mentors to share positive accomplishments of protégés with others.

Highlighting collaborative projects by mentor partnerships in a school newsletter, bulletin board or staff meeting.

Constructing a Wall of Fame in a school hallway, workroom or library. This wall could contain pictures and notes regarding accomplishments and efforts by individuals, groups, grade levels, protégés, mentors and other staff.

Setting aside time at the last staff meeting of the year to highlight staff accomplishments by grade level.

Extensions

Include these successes in parent newsletters and at parent meetings such as PTA or PTO.

Include a Wall of Fame for the system at a school board meeting.

Recognize collaborative projects that involve staff from more than one school in a special section of the Wall of Fame, newsletter or bulletin boards.

Tip

Ask both staff and students to nominate distinguished colleagues at designated times throughout the year; perhaps in October, January, March and May. This practice allows for a variety of activities throughout the year, not just at the end.

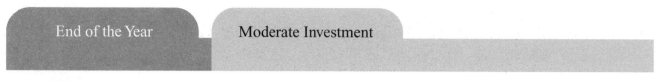

End of the Year   Moderate Investment

'Aha' Chart

Purpose: To efficiently capture and share reflections and learnings for both protégés and mentors.

Ask protégés to complete an 'Aha' chart or log to be shared with future protégés. This technique reinforces the notion of continuing to learn from our experiences and collectively increasing the professional knowledge base.

	Beginning of Year	Middle of Year	End of Year
I am glad I knew . . .			
I wish I had known . . .			
I am still wondering . . .			

Extensions
Complete the chart for at least the first two years of service.

Ask mentors to complete the chart regarding their mentoring experience.

Use the 'I am still wondering . . .' stem as data for providing information and resources in the future.

Tips
Collect, synthesize and distribute a summary chart for other staff.

Include this activity during Collaborative Role-Alike Support. Group meetings (see page 92) at appropriate times of the year to ensure time for reflection.

Learning at All Levels

Purpose: To encourage collaborations among both students and staff.

This strategy invites the protégé and mentor to collaboratively plan a project or unit for completion by students in each classroom.

Brainstorm possible projects or units that would be of high interest and directly relate to student outcomes.

Devise a plan of action, identifying resources, responsibilities, timelines and other staff that might be needed or involved.

Prepare students for the project and the collaborative activites.

At the end of the project, jointly celebrate the results.

Extensions

Debrief the project at several levels; learning from the project (students and staff) and learning from working with each other.

Plan a joint field trip to enhance the learning.

Tips

Choose a unit or topic of high interest to both colleagues and students.

Select a topic that allows the protégé to contribute equally.

Tips Too Good To Leave Out

Just a few more ideas too good to leave out, organized as timesavers, learning opportunities, relationship builders and additional support.

Timesavers

Provide printed regulations, policies and procedures with highlights or annotations.

Suggest that your protégé keep an ongoing list of questions/needs in classroom.

Jointly construct a calendar with red letter days and 'high jam' periods.

Order supplies before they are needed.

Anticipate likely concerns and problems. Create a 'life-saver' file of practical ideas to address them.

Learning Opportunities

Provide small amounts of information as needed. Avoid doing 'an information dump.'

Plan for Problem-Solving Partners Sessions (at least 3 per year) where each person has a presenting problem and you jointly engage in brainstorming, assessing options, decision-making (see page 91).

Seek opportunities to collaborate with your protégé and arrange for observation opportunities.

Arrange for 'practice' assessment observations by a peer or the mentor to familiarize the protégé with the process.

Model teaching procedures and 'think aloud' with the protégé about your choice points, criteria for selecting strategies and personal learnings from a teaching experience.

Duplicate and share resource files containing ideas and activities for activating and integrating content.

Relationship Builders

Mentors should share challenges faced and strategies used to overcome barriers.

Conduct a conference while taking a walk, sitting outside, etc. to reduce stress.

Model trustworthy behavior/confidentiality.

Attend to stress management strategies.

Develop common and shared vocabulary.

Seek opportunities to grow together and move across the continuum from consultant to coach.

Additional Support

Leave notes of encouragement and support, particularly during the first two weeks of school and during times of intensive paperwork/reporting requirements.

Trade professional articles of interest; highlight important points first.

Accompany protégé on the first non-teaching assignment.

Introduce protégé to support services staff and provide information on available services.

Assist with identifying special needs students in the protégé's classroom.

Section 7   Appendix

This section provides a selection of materials to enhance and supplement the body of this handbook. Included in this Appendix you will find:

MENTORING RELATIONSHIP: SELF-ASSESSMENT RUBRIC

This scale for assessing the quality and effectiveness of the mentor/protégé relationship is organized into four levels, with Level Four describing highly effective, learning-focused mentoring. Use this rubric to establish clear expectations, parameters and goals for your mentor/protégé relationship.

MENTOR'S SKILLS: PRIMARY TRAIT RUBRIC

This self-assessment tool provides baseline data and serves to support skill goal-setting for both novice and experienced mentors. The rubric identifies specific verbal and non-verbal skill sets that enhance a mentor's effectiveness. The three level scale ranges from a lack of awareness to fluent and flexible application of the learning-focused mentor's toolkit.

TEACHING AND LEARNING PORTFOLIO

This section details the value of and process for developing a Teaching and Learning Portfolio. All the necessary forms for this process can be found in Section Eight, Structured Forms, Tools and Blacklines.

TEACHING AND LEARNING PORTFOLIO: ASSESSMENT RUBRICS

A four-point scale for collaboratively assessing the Teaching and Learning Portfolio.

INTERSTATE NEW TEACHER ASSESSMENT AND SUPPORT CONSORTIUM (INTASC) STANDARDS FOR BEGINNING TEACHERS

Ten nationally recognized standards for excellence in teaching designed to guide goal setting and reflection for novices. Use these standards to guide and ground learning-focused conversations.

FREQUENTLY ASKED QUESTIONS: ISSUES AND POSSIBILITIES

FAQs regarding logistical factors in mentor programs that effect mentors' capacity to serve their proteges. The questions are organized by issues; and we suggest a number of possibilities for addressing each area.

MiraVia, LLC 3 Lost Acre Trail Sherman CT 06784 860.354.4543   www.miravia.com

Mentoring Relationship: Self-Assessment Rubric

Rubrics are a useful way to identify and qualify the desired characteristics of a mentoring relationship. Use this inventory to self-assess the developing mentor/protégé relationship. Choose the level that represents the best fit, rather than expecting an exact match with each statement.

Level Four

Contact between mentor and protégé is scheduled frequently, protected from competing demands and meets the mutual needs of the partnership as well as advancing the goals of the district.

Both the mentor and the protégé consistently initiate learning-focused conversations regarding teacher and student learning.

The mentor demonstrates versatility in appropriately consulting, collaborating and coaching to purposefully develop the protégé's capacity to generate information.

Mentoring interactions promote connection making between instructional practice and student results. Personal learnings are transferred and applied to other content and contexts. These learnings inform future actions.

The mentor models problem-solving processes and reflective practice which protégés adopt.

The protégé participates in school-wide goal achievement and gradually interacts as a collective member of the professional school community.

Level Three

The mentor and protégé maintain regular contact.

Interactions promote collaboration through joint planning, problem-solving, decision-making and reciprocity of learning results.

The mentoring relationship is mutually beneficial and information production is equal.

Learning-focused conversations center on the implementation of curriculum and generally recognized best practice.

The mentor provides connections with grade level/content area colleagues and promotes collaborative opportunities.

Mentoring Relationship: Self-Assessment Rubric *(continued)*

Level Two

Contact occurs as scheduled and satisfies the protégé's needs for information.

Throughout the relationship, information production remains higher for the mentor.

The mentor conducts conferences employing strategies to fix current problems and add to the protégé's list of activities.

Discussions center on specific episodes and situations. Meeting protégé needs may become time intensive for the mentor.

The mentor provides orientation and introduction to the professional school community.

Level One

Mentor-protégé contact is irregular and generally precipitated by a need for information or assistance.

Interactions are limited to the transfer of critical, basic information.

The mentor provides suggestions and advice as requested.

The protégé's collegial and collaborative opportunities are limited to other novices or professionals close in proximity or content specialty.

The greatest learnings for the protégé are within the management domain and generally do not progress to the examination of impact.

Survival strategies are the emphasis of the protégé's learning.

Mentor's Skills: Primary Trait Rubric

Purpose: This self-assessment scale organizes specific attributes and skills for each element of the linguistic toolkit. It provides baseline data for goal-setting and a convenient way to identify strong skills and areas for development.

Applications: Use this rubric to identify goals and monitor programs.

Directions:

1. Complete the Rubric without the aid of any print materials.

2. For the skills that you rated 'unaware', use the text to learn more about that skill.

3. Set and record learning goals; add some strategies for skill development, as well.

4. Revisit the rubric at regular intervals, perhaps every other month, to monitor your progress.

Variations: Use this rubric with a Study Buddy. Set goals and agree to practice and share strategies for success throughout the school year.

Tip: Use this rubric in combination with a video. Tape yourself conducting a learning-focused conversation. Watch the videotape; then rate your skills. If possible, tape several conversations for a richer data pool.

MiraVia, LLC 3 Lost Acre Trail Sherman CT 06784 860.354.4543 www.miravia.com

Mentor's Skills: Primary Traits Rubric *(continued)*

Name _____ **Date** _____

Attending Fully	Unaware	With Conscious Competency	Flexibly and Fluently
Apply physical alignment			
Matching posture			
Matching gesture			
Physical referencing			
Matching breathing (depth, duration, rate)			
Apply vocal alignment			
Matching intonational patterns (volume, inflection)			
Matching pace of language			
Attending to word choice/with intentional match or mismatch			
Able to recover when focus is lost			

Attending Fully	Unaware	With Conscious Competency	Flexibly and Fluently
Listen to understand			
Listen without interruption			
Listen non-judgmentally, without • personal referencing • personal curiosity • personal certainty			
Listen for assumptions, inferences, problem frame, perceptions, perspectives			

MiraVia, LLC 3 Lost Acre Trail Sherman CT 06784 860.354.4543   www.miravia.com

Mentor's Skills: Primary Traits Rubric *(continued)*

Inviting Thinking	Unaware	With Conscious Competency	Flexibly and Fluently
Use invitational stems which include:			
An approachable voice (intonation)			
Plural forms			
Exploratory language			
Presume positive intention			
Maintain non-judgmental stance			
Embed positive presuppositions			

Sustaining Thinking	Unaware	With Conscious Competency	Flexibly and Fluently
Pause/ Use Silence			
Pause to allow time for thought • after asking a question • after hearing a response to allow for additional information • before making a response or asking a question			
Paraphrase			
Apply paraphrase within a pattern of pause/paraphrase/question			
Apply paraphrases that: • acknowledge and clarify emotion • acknowledge and clarify content • summarize/organize comment • shift level of abstraction			

Mentor's Skills: Primary Traits Rubric *(continued)*

Sustaining Thinking *(continued)*	Unaware	With Conscious Competency	Flexibly and Fluently
Inquire—to open thinking			
Use nondichotomous forms (no yes/no)			
Use language to focus on specific cognitive processes			
Invite metacognitive thinking			
Ask questions that produce new insights and applications			
Probe—to focus thinking			
Ask questions to clarify explanations, ideas, anecdotes, generalizations			
Ask questions to examine inferences, assumptions, implications, consequences			
Surface specific examples, non-examples			

Teaching and Learning Portfolio

Developing a teaching portfolio with your protégé structures a rich source of data for learning-focused mentoring. The new teacher's portfolio can be related to, or developed in conjunction with, the portfolio sometimes required for personnel evaluation.

During the first year of teaching, the portfolio should be viewed as a scrapbook or container organizing significant artifacts and noting specific accomplishments from which to grow. This developmental process will surface relevant information and products that can be used to inform and guide future professional practice.

The following are suggested steps in the portfolio process. Mentor and protégé may choose to follow the formal steps in creating a teaching and learning portfolio, engaging a support team. Or, they may choose or adapt elements of the process that will best serve learning needs and choices. The asterisks(*) indicate forms provided in Section Eight, Structured Forms, Tools and Blacklines.

Identify a support team.
> Include the mentor, and at least one other educator to collaborate with the protégé during portfolio construction and throughout the first year of teaching.

Conduct an initial planning meeting.
> The protégé meets with the support team to discuss identified student goals and share the initial Self-Assessment Reflection (*). The protégé and the team will explore professional knowledge and skills needed to ensure achievement of student goals.

Create a learning-focused growth plan.
> The protégé finalizes a Learning-Focused Growth Plan (*) and shares it. This step begins the monitoring of the Learning-Focused Growth Cycle.

Regular reflection.
> The protégé may record daily reflections in a log or the plan book noting details and incidents. Each week, a more formal structured reflection is composed as a Reflection Journal: Weekly Entry (*).

Collect and select additional artifacts.
> Biweekly, the protégé selects from a collection of potential portfolio artifacts, retaining those that are relevant to the Learning-Focused Growth Plan and purging others.

Conduct monthly support sessions.
> The protégé meets monthly with the mentor, or at least one member of the support team, to review and discuss progress and identify needed resources.

Conduct interim support team meeting.
The entire team meets with the protégé at the end of the first semester to share progress, revise and/or add growth goals and determine additional needs for support.

Present the portfolio.
The protégé presents the portfolio, providing a summary of learnings to the support team. The team and the protégé develop plans for continued learning during the coming year.

Teaching and Learning Portfolio: Assessment Rubrics

Use the following scale to assess the Teaching and Learning Portfolio.

Level 4

Portfolio requirements have been completed. Selected artifacts clearly illustrate growth/learnings. Professional goals are connected to the identified goal(s) for student learning.

The Action Option steps demonstrate a strong relationship to national or local standards of practice and district initiatives and reforms.

Structured reflections reveal insights regarding student and teacher learnings that are used to inform future practice.

There is a clear focus on interpreting student results and making connections to teacher actions, instructional strategies, curriculum materials, etc.

Instructional techniques emphasize cross-curricular and authentic applications.

The portfolio includes evidence of varied resources (within and outside the school/school system) and collaborations to support goal attainment.

Level 3

Portfolio requirements have been completed. Selected artifacts indicate growth and the identification of learnings.

There is a tie between expected outcomes for students and professional goals. District expectations for student learning and teacher performance are congruent with identified personal expectations.

Steps included in the Action Options are logical and reasonable for goal achievement and demonstrate attention to local or national standards of practice.

Reflections reveal examination of multiple variables for outcomes.

Appropriate resources for goal achievement include the professional community.

Level 2

Portfolio requirements are complete. Selected artifacts relate to goals; however, they do not clearly identify the growth and/or learnings from the experience.

Outcomes are identified for students along with professional goals. Local standards for teacher practice and student learning are addressed.

Reflections reveal insights about student learning and teacher learning; but may not always make clear connections between actions and results.

Resources are identified to assist in implementation of strategies/activities. Personal and district expectations for students and teachers are aligned.

Level 1

Portfolio requirements are not complete.

Artifacts are included and relate to identified goals. Student and teacher goals have been identified; but are not clearly related.

Reflections attend to achievement of outcomes; but show consideration of primarily external variables.

Personal learnings tend to be episodic and are not consistently used to identify patterns and surface possible generalizations to inform future practice.

Resources have been identified; but may be limited in scope.

INTASC:
Standards for Beginning Teachers

INTASC, or Interstate New Teacher Assessment and Support Consortium, has identified ten standards reflecting requisite knowledge and skills for beginning teachers. Input from state education agencies, higher education institutions and national education organizations was used in formulating the INTASC standards. These standards, along with district standards, may be considered when determining areas to strengthen or a focus for growth.

Standard 1: Knowledge of Subject Matter
> The teacher understands the central concepts, tools of inquiry and structures of the disciplines he or she teaches and can create learning experiences that make these aspects of subject matter meaningful for students.

Standard 2: Knowledge of Human Development and Learning
> The teacher understands how children learn and develop, and can provide learning opportunities that support a child's intellectual, social and personal development.

Standard 3: Adapting Instruction for Individual Needs
> The teacher understands how students differ in their approaches to learning and creates instructional opportunities that are adapted to diverse learners.

Standard 4: Multiple Instructional Strategies
> The teacher understands and uses a variety of instructional strategies to encourage student development of critical thinking, problem-solving and performance skills.

Standard 5: Classroom Motivation and Management Skills
> The teacher uses an understanding of individual and group motivation and behavior to create a learning environment that encourages positive social interaction, active engagement in learning and self-motivation.

Standard 6: Communication Skills
> The teacher uses knowledge of effective verbal, nonverbal and media communication techniques to foster active inquiry, collaboration and supportive interaction in the classroom.

Standard 7: Instructional Planning Skills
> The teacher plans instruction based upon knowledge of subject matter, students, the community and curriculum goals.

Standard 8: Assessment of Student Learning

    The teacher understands and uses formal and informal assessment strategies to evaluate and ensure the continuous intellectual, social and physical development of the learner.

Standard 9: Professional Commitment and Responsibility

    The teacher is a reflective practitioner who continually evaluates the effects of his or her choices and actions on others (students, parents and other professionals in the learning community); and who actively seeks out opportunities to grow professionally.

Standard 10: Partnerships

    The teacher fosters relationships with school colleagues, parents and agencies in the larger community to support students' learning and well being.

Frequently Asked Questions: Issues and Possiblities

Issue:

We can't perfectly match mentors and protégés.

What might we do to create appropriate partners?

Possibilities:

Protégés and mentors should be thoughtfully paired considering criteria such as grade level, subject area content and accessibility (including physical proximity and availability of time). While many mentors feel they can best serve the new teacher who has the same job functions as their own, reality rarely provides for perfect matching.

   Consider developing a mentoring team. Teams might include system-wide personnel, counselors, library-media specialists, and a cross-section of experienced teachers including special needs, bilingual and literacy support.

   Assign a site-based mentor along with a content support mentor from the central office or another location.

Mentors of protégés teaching in significantly different content areas or grade levels might:

   Connect the protégé with a colleague or a network of colleagues that can attend to curricular/behavioral issues, questions or concerns.

   Use grade level or department chairs to assist.

   Encourage collaborative and collegial sharing during protégé support sessions.

Mentors of protégés not located in close proximity might:

   Use the Mindful Memorandums (see Section Eight, Structured Forms, Tools and Blacklines) and other methods of correspondence to record protégé's questions, issues ideas and requests—and the mentor's timely responses.

   Communicate regularly by e-mail, telephone and/or school mail.

   Share unit and lesson plans and other curriculum materials in advance, preserving meeting time for focused questions.

   Record topics for discussion to be addressed at the next informal opportunity or scheduled meeting.

   Arrange for someone who is physically closer to the protégé to be the 'go-to' for immediate needs.

Frequently Asked Questions: Issues and Possiblities *(continued)*

Schedule regular meetings and place high value on honoring the commitment.

Remember, it is more important to provide learning-focused mentoring (fully attending, balancing challenge with support, maintaining relationship) than it is to create ideal pairs.

Issue:
We have many more new teachers than available mentors.

How can we make the best use of our resources?

Possibilities:
For more efficient use of time and energy:

Schedule individual meetings as well as group sessions for appropriate topics.

Network colleagues to provide additional support.

Recruit retired educators to serve in a mentoring capacity.

Encourage support sessions among protégés to share ideas and materials.

Create an Idea Bank (see Section One, The Mentor's Role) to address similar problems that may emerge.

Issue:
There is never enough time to meet everyone's needs.

How can we maximize our use of time?

Possibilities:
Time is our scarcest resource. This issue may be the most challenging of all. One consideration is that while accessibility is a critical component, it does not have to be defined strictly as formal conferences. Additionally, advanced preparation will make better use of conference time. Consider these possibilities when arranging for regular communication:

Schedule at least one uninterrupted, structured, learning-focused conversation each month, focusing on instructional issues.

Construct the optimal schedule for meetings with your protégé.

Brainstorm possibilities and designate meeting dates. This schedule will need to be revisited every four to five weeks to check for continued availability. Remember to balance personal and professional life for both parties.

MiraVia, LLC 3 Lost Acre Trail Sherman CT 06784 860.354.4543 www.miravia.com

Frequently Asked Questions: Issues and Possiblities *(continued)*

As topics and questions arise, the mentor and protégé each should consider the most appropriate forum to address them—a conference or an alternative form of communication such as Double-Entry Journal, e-mail communications or a brief note in the mailbox. Prioritize needs and address the most critical first.

Make occasional but consistent check-ins to provide an opportunity for informal sharing.

Utilize e-mail, notes in mailboxes, telephone conversations and school mail to maintain communication (see Section Eight, Structured Forms, Tools and Blacklines; Mindful Memorandum, Form L).

Take advantage of Problem-Solving Partnership meetings (see Section Five, Facilitating Professional Vision) where each partner offers a problem or question.

Note: *Find additional ideas for addressing this issue in Section Three, Maximizing Time and Attention.*

Issue:
We need clear data sources for assessing the mentoring program.

What are some tools that are time and cost effective?

Possibilities:
Assessment tools should measure the goals of the program and tap a variety of data sources.

Identify examples of archival data sources: beginning teacher retention rates, student performance scores, professional development records or logs of parent contacts.

Construct collectible data sources including reflection logs, dialogue journals, observation notes, records of contacts between mentors and protégés.

Tap multiple perspectives through protégé surveys, mentor surveys and administrator surveys. When appropriate, include student and parent perspectives.

Note: *Many of the forms included in this handbook can be formalized to provide feedback regarding the program. Examples include the Mentoring Relationship Assessment Rubric, the Learning-Focused Growth Plan and related Tracking Progress Form and the structured Reflection Journals.*

Section 8   Structured Forms, Tools and Blacklines

T he forms in this section can be used as portfolio items or as independent tools that can serve similar functions in supporting rigor and reflection. Either way, each can be individualized to address the goals of the protégé or the district. Use these blackline masters to produce as many copies as necessary for your work. This section includes:

STUDENT GOALS WORKSHEET

FORM A

What are three major goals for student learning this year? Consider major district initiatives and grade level/content curriculum guides. (Example: Students will use technology for research, communication and organization.) Gaining expertise in management (student and resource) is always prominent on novices' lists of 'need-to-know.' Attention to student goals focuses the novice on essential content and instructional skills and knowledge.

INITIAL SELF-ASSESSMENT PROFILE

FORM B

Completion of the Initial Self-Assessment provides the opportunity to reflect on past experiences and surface current concerns and questions. Goals for learning should be reasonable, practical and related to the students' goals.

BEGINNING TEACHING SELF-ASSESSMENT INVENTORY

FORM C

This Self-Assessment Inventory is based on a synthesis of research studies on the perceived needs of beginning teachers. Completion of this survey increases awareness, facilitates goal-setting and normalizes the insecurities and concerns of novices as they face their first year of teaching.

LEARNING-FOCUSED GROWTH PLAN

FORM D

As a major component of a Learning-Focused Growth Cycle, the Growth Plan promotes a formal commitment between the mentor and the protégé. It articulates clear expectations and Action Options for accomplishing goals. This plan is constructed according to the most pressing needs of the protégé and contains no magic number for goals or action steps. Protégés and mentors are cautioned to keep the plan reasonable and useful. It is important that completion of the goals does not become unattainable or overwhleming. The plan is an organizational tool and a guide for selecting the most promising professional development activities, readings and learning opportunities for maximum growth.

MiraVia, LLC 3 Lost Acre Trail Sherman CT 06784 860.354.4543   www.miravia.com

FORM E   LEARNING-FOCUSED GROWTH
PLAN: TRACKING PROGRESS

A useful structure for recording key points and learnings during the Growth Cycle, theTracking Progress page is used to keep an informal record of significant actions (practice opportunities, mentor sessions, observations of others, etc.), capture insights and note questions for further exploration. This information provides a focus for mentor sessions and develops inquiry-based practice.

FORMS F-K   REFLECTION JOURNAL

Engaging in structured reflections provides a developmental view of progress. Keeping a journal begins a lifelong journey of reflective practice. In these pages, specific prompts are provided for weekly reflections to support protégés as they move through the stages of concern identified by Frances Fuller's research: *Self* (personal concerns), *Task* (issues of management and implementation) and *Impact* (concern for the impact of practice on others, including students, colleagues and the school community.)

FORM L   MINDFUL MEMORANDUM

There will be times during the year when it is difficult to arrange a face-to-face meeting with your protégé. The Mindful Memorandum is a timely tool for communicating without a formal meeting. Note the scale for prioritizing urgency. Use this form to invite requests for support or sharing of information that can be conveyed in a memo.

FORM M   LEARNING-FOCUSED VERBAL
TOOLKIT: POCKET FILES

As you develop increasing fluency with the learning-focused toolkit, these pocket files can serve to support your learning. You might want to cut out the tool note files and focus on a specific tool during your interaction(s)—or keep the full page handy while talking with your protégé.

Student Goals Worksheet

At least three major goals for student learning this year include:

Connections between these goals and district/school initiatives include:
(Examples: District Math Initiative, Grade Level Curriculum Requirement, etc.)

MiraVia, LLC 3 Lost Acre Trail Sherman CT 06784 860.354.4543   www.miravia.com

Initial Self-Assessment Profile/Stem Completion

In thinking about my student/previous teaching experience, my most vivid recollection is . . .

I am confident in my ability to . . .

Critical areas to focus my learning include . . .

During this year, I am looking forward to . . .

Anticipating this year, I am most concerned about . . .

MiraVia, LLC 3 Lost Acre Trail Sherman CT 06784 860.354.4543   www.miravia.com

FORM B

Beginning Teacher Self-Assessment Inventory

In the areas below, please indicate the response for each item that best matches your concern/need level. Use this inventory with your mentor to determine some areas for support, identify resources and set learning goals.

1. I am really anxious about this.
2. I'm okay, but it would be good to talk about this.
3. I've got this under control, at least for now.

Information About Policy and Procedures

____The teacher-evaluation system

____Paperwork and deadlines

____Expectations of the principal

____Expectations of my colleagues

____Communicating with parents

____Standardized tests

Working with Students

____Establishing classroom routines

____Motivating reluctant learners

____Maintaining student discipline

____Assessing student needs

____Differentiating instruction for individual learners

____Implementing the curriculum

____Evaluating student progress

Accessing Resources

____Organizing/setting up my classroom

____Accessing instructional materials and resources

____Arranging field trips

____Ordering materials

____Using the library and media resources

____Working with special services

Managing Time

____Organizing my day/week

____Lesson planning

____Following the daily/weekly schedule

____Attending meetings

____Supervising extracurricular activities

____Opportunity for professional development

____Maintaining personal/ professional balance

Considerations for our mentor/protégé relationship:

Other areas I'd like to address:

MiraVia, LLC 3 Lost Acre Trail Sherman CT 06784 860.354.4543   www.miravia.com

Learning-Focused Growth Plan

Focus for Growth: What do I want to know/be able to do?   **Target Completion Date** _____

Filling the Knowledge Gap: How and where will I learn about it? (readings, videos, talk to experts, etc.) How will I build my skill level?

Implementation Steps:
When and how will I use the new information/skill(s)?

Assessment/Data Collection: How will I know that I am appropriately implementing new information/skill(s)? To what degree is this new information/skill(s) producing desired student results?

Assistance Options: What resources might I need? What resources are available to me?

Learning-Focused Growth Plan:Tracking Progress

Date	Action

Key Learnings	New Questions

Date	Action

Key Learnings	New Questions

MiraVia, LLC 3 Lost Acre Trail Sherman CT 06784 860.354.4543   www.miravia.com

Reflection Journal I   Date: Concern Focus: SELF

Significant events for me this week were . . .

As a result of these events, I have learned . . .

I realize that I need to know more about . . .

This week I am most proud of my . . .

Information Needs	Resource/Material Needs

Reflection Journal II   Date:

Concern Focus: SELF

I am excited by the opportunity to . . .

I have noticed that I am doing well with . . .

I am curious about . . .

By the end of this semester, I want to be able to . . .

Information Needs	Resource/Material Needs

MiraVia, LLC 3 Lost Acre Trail Sherman CT 06784 860.354.4543   www.miravia.com

Reflection Journal III   Date: Concern Focus: TASK

Reflecting on my classroom management, I realize that
    when I . . .

    my students . . .

Strategies I want to remember include . . .

At this point, I know I can control . . .

By the end of the year, I will be able to . . .

Information Needs	Resource/Material Needs

MiraVia, LLC 3 Lost Acre Trail Sherman CT 06784 860.354.4543 www.miravia.com

FORM H

Reflection Journal IV   Date: Concern Focus: TASK

Regarding my use of time, I have noticed . . .

I am pleased when I . . .

Managing paperwork and other tasks is easier for me when . . .

My biggest question about feeling professionally in control is . . .

Information Needs	Resource/Material Needs

Reflection Journal V   Date:

Concern Focus: IMPACT

As a result of my instruction this week, my students can . . .

For my class, I am thinking about the following changes in curriculum . . .

If I could relive one day or class this week, it would be . . .

Given what I know now, I would change . . .

Information Needs	Resource/Material Needs

MiraVia, LLC 3 Lost Acre Trail Sherman CT 06784 860.354.4543   www.miravia.com

Form J

Reflection Journal VI   Date: Concern Focus: TASK

The most important lesson I've learned this year is . . .

In thinking about other colleagues, it would be interesting to work
with . . .

on . . .

I can contribute to the professional school community by . . .

In thinking about school goals and projects, I need to know more about . . .

Information Needs	Resource/Material Needs

Mindful Memorandum

Mindful Memorandum   To: From: Date:

Hottest Topic of the Moment:

Questions/Concerns/Successes

Priority Gauge:

☐ Need To Talk Now!   ☐ When You Can, But Soon   ☐ Whenever

Mentor's Response

To: From: Date:

Response/Comments:

Learning-Focused Verbal Toolkit

- ## Pause
- ## Paraphrase
- ## Inquire
- ## Probe
- ## Extend

Pausing

Allow time for thinking, elaborating and framing your own thoughts and responses. Three critical occasions for pausing produce a conversation paced for thoughtfulness:

- After asking a question
- After receiving a response
- While you frame your own language (note: this pause often occurs between the paraphrase and the next question)

Paraphrasing

Signal listening, determine understanding and support thinking with these paraphrase forms:

Acknowledge/ Clarify—calibrating content and emotions

Summarize/Organize—a statement of themes, big ideas and separation of confusing or jumbled issues

Shift Level of Abstraction—a shift in logical level, raised to a category or conceptual label or focused as a concrete example

Inquiring

Support your partner's learning with open-ended questions, keeping these criteria in mind:

- Ask without judgments (if you have a preferred response- it's not inquiry!)

- Use an approachable intonation and syntax that invites multiple responses

- Focus on cognition that supports and enhances meaning-making

Probing

Ask questions that clarify vague language, explore details and generate examples. Increase focus and precision of thinking by asking for specific examples regarding:
- Who
- What
- When
- Where
- How

Extending

Make data available for making discoveries and developing new understandings by:

- Giving information
- Framing expectations
- Providing resources

Section 9   References and Resources

Asian-Pacific Economic Cooperation. (1997). *Overview of teacher induction policy and practice: Results of the exploratory survey.* (Issue brief No. 97-HR-01.1). Washington, DC: Asian-Pacific Economic Cooperation.

Ballou, D., and Podgursky, M. (1997). Reforming teacher training and recruitment. *Government Union Review, 17* (4), 1-47.

Bandler, R., & Grinder, J. (1971). *The structure of magic.* Palo Alto, CA: Science and Behavior Books.

Bransford, J., Brown, A., & Cocking, R. (Eds) (1999). *How people learn: Brain, mind, experience, and school.* Washington DC: National Research Council.

Bridges, E. (1990). Evaluation for tenure & dismissal. In J. Millman & L. Darling-Hammond (Eds.), *The new handbook of teacher evaluation: Assessing elementary & secondary teachers.* Newbury Park, CA: Sage: 147-157.

Bullough, R. (1989). *First-year teacher: A case study.* New York: Teachers College Press.

Calderhead, J. (1996). Teachers: Beliefs and knowledge. In D. Berliner & R.C. Calfee (Eds.), *Handbook of Educational Psychology* (pp. 709-725). New York: Simon & Schuster Macmillan.

Carlson, W.S. (1993). Teacher knowledge and discourse control: Quantitative evidence from novice biology teachers' classrooms. *Journal of Research in Science Teaching, 30* (5), 471-481.

Center for Cognitive Coaching. P.O. Box 260860, Highlands Ranch, CO, 80163, p. (303) 683-6146, f. (303) 791-1772 www.cognitivecoaching.com

Chang, F. Y. (1994). Schoolteachers' moral reasoning. In R. Houston (Ed). *Handbook of research on teacher education* (pp. 291-310). New York: Macmillan.

Chester, M. D. & Beaudin, B. Q. (1996). Efficacy beliefs of newly hired teachers in urban schools. *American Educational Research Journal, 33*(1), 233-257.

Clark, C.M. & Peterson, P.L. (1986). Teacher thought processes. In M.C. Whittrock (Ed). *Handbook of research on teaching* (3rd ed) (pp. 255-296). New York: Macmillan.

Cogan, M. L. (1973). *Clinical supervision.* Boston: Houghton Mifflin.

Costa, A. & Garmston, R. (1985). Supervision for intelligent teaching. *Educational Leadership. 42* (7), 70-80.

Costa, A. & Garmston, R. (2002). *Cognitive Coaching: A foundation for renaissance schools.* Norwood, MA: Christopher Gordon Publishers, Inc.

Covert, J., Williams, L. & Kennedy, W. (1991). Some perceived professional needs of beginning teachers in Newfoundland. *The Alberta Journal of Educational Administration, 27* (1), 3-17.

Dagenais, Raymond J. (1995). *Some tentative mentoring program standards.* The Mentoring Leadership and Resource Network.

Daloz, Laurent A. (1999). *Mentor: Guiding the journey of adult learners.* San Francisco: Jossey-Bass.

Darling-Hammond, L., and McLaughlin, M.V. (1996). Policies that support professional development in an era of reform. *Teacher learning: New policies and practices,* Mclaughlin, M.V. & Oberman, I., (Eds). New York: Teachers College Press.

Darling-Hammond, L. (1996). The quiet revolution: rethinking teacher development. *Educational Leadership, 53* (6), 4-11.

Darling-Hammond, L. (1997). *The right to learn.* San Francisco: Jossey-Bass.

Darling-Hammond, L. (1998). Teachers and teaching: Testing policy hypotheses from a national commission report. *Educational Researcher, 27* (1), 5-15.

Elgin, S. H. (2000). *The gentle art of verbal self-defense.* New York: Prentice-Hall.

Erikson, E. (1982). *The life cycle completed.* New York: Norton.

Eisner, E.W. (1994). *The educational imagination: On the design and evaluation of school programs.* New York: Macmillan.

Feiman-Nemser, S., Carver, C., Schwille, S., & Yusko, B. (1999). Beyond support: Taking new teachers seriously as learners. M. Scherer (Ed.) *A Better Beginning* (pp. 3-12). Alexandria VA: Association for Supervision and Curriculum Development.

Fessler, R. & Christensen, J. (1992). *The teacher career cycle: Understanding and guiding the professional development of teachers.* Boston: Allyn & Bacon.

Feuerstein, R. & Feuerstein, S. (1991). Mediated learning experience: A theoretical review, in Feuerstein, T., Klein, P.S., & Tannenbaum A. (Eds) *A Mediate Learning Experience* (pp. 213-240). London: Freund Publishing House.

Fuller, F. (1969). Concerns of teachers: A developmental conceptualization. *American Education Research Journal, 6*(2), 207-226.

Galvez-Hjornevik, C. (1986). Mentoring among teachers: A review of literature. (Report No. SPO26700). Austin, TX: *Journal of Teacher Education.* (ERIC No. ED 262 032).

Ganser, Tom (1994). *The impact of time and place in mentoring.* Whitewater, WI: University of Wisconsin.

Garmston, R.; Linder, C. & Whitaker, J. (1993). Reflections on Cognitive Coaching. *Educational Leadership: 51* (2), 57-61.

Gilligan, C. (1982). *In a different voice.* Cambridge, MA: Harvard University Press.

Glickman, C., Gordon, S., & Ross-Gordon, J. (1995). *Supervision of instruction* (3rd ed.). Boston: Allyn & Bacon.

Gold, Y. (1996). Beginning teacher support: Attrition, mentoring & induction. In J. Sikula (Ed.), *Second handbook of research on teacher education* (pp. 548-594). New York: Macmillan.

Guild, P. B. & Garger, S. (1998). *Marching to different drummers.* Alexandria, VA: Association for Supervision and Curriculum Development.

Grinder, M. (1995). *ENVOY: A personal guide to classroom management.* Battleground, WA: Michael Grinder and Associates.

Huling-Austin, L. (1990). Teacher induction programs and internships. In R. Houston (Ed.), *Handbook of research on teacher education* (pp. 535-548). New York: MacMillan.

Huling-Austin, L., Putman, S., & Galvey-Hjornevik (1986). *Model teacher induction project study findings.* (Report No. 7212). Austin, TX: University of Texas at Austin, R & D Center for Teacher Education.

Hunt, D. (1971). *Matching models of education.* Toronto, Ontario: Institute for Studies in Education.

Hunt, D.E. (1976). Teachers' adaptation: Reading and flexing to students. *Journal of Teacher Education, 27*, 268-275.

Hunt, D.E. (1981). Teachers' adaptation: Reading and flexing to students. In B. Joyce, C. Brown, & L. Peck (Eds.). *Flexibility in teaching*. New York: Longman: 59-71.

Ingersoll, R. (June 1998). *The problem of out-of-field teaching*. [online]. http://www.pdkintl.org/kappan/king9806.htm

Interstate New Teacher Assessment and Support Consortium (1995). INTASC Core Standards. [online]. http://develop.ccsso.cybercentral.com/intasc.htm

Jones, V. (1996). Classroom management. In *Handbook of research on teacher education,* J. P. Sikula, T. J. Buttery, and E. Guyton (Eds). New York: Simon & Schuster Macmillan.

Joyce, B., & Showers, B. (1995). *Student achievement through staff development* (2nd ed.). New York: Longman.

Joyce, B., & Weil, M. (1996). *Models of teaching*. Englewood Cliffs, NJ: Prentice-Hall.

King, S. H., & Bey, T. M. The need for urban teacher mentors. *Education and Urban Society, 28* (1), 3-10.

King, P, & Kitchener, K. (1994). *Developing reflective judgment: Understanding and promoting intellectual growth and critical thinking in adolescents and adults*. San Francisco: Jossey-Bass.

Lee, O., & Fradd, S.H. (1998). Science for all, including students from non-English-language background. *Educational Researcher, 27* (4), 12-21.

Lipton, L., & Wellman, B. (2000). *Pathways to understanding: Patterns and practices in the learning-focused classroom.* Guilford, VT: Pathways Publishing.

Marzano, R. J. (1992). *A different kind of classroom: Teaching with dimensions of learning.* Alexandria, VA: Association for Supervision and Curriculum Development.

Marzano, R.J., Pickering, D.J., & Pollock, E. (2001). *Classroom instruction that works: Research-based strategies for increasing student achievement.* Alexandria, VA: Association for Supervision and Curriculum Development.

McAllister, G. & Irvine, J.J. (2000). Cross cultural competency and multicultural teacher education. *Review of Educational Research, 70* (1), 3-24.

McLaughlin, M.; Vogt, M.; Anderson, J.; Dumez, J.; Peter, M. & Hunter, A. (1998) *Portfolio models: Reflections across the teaching profession.* Norwood, MA: Christopher-Gordon Publishers, Inc.

Moir, E. (1999). The stages of a teacher's first year. In M. Scherer (Ed.) *Better beginnings: Supporting and mentoring new teachers* (pp. 19-23). Alexandria, VA: Association for Supervision and Curriculum Development.

National Center for Research on Teacher Learning (1999). *Findings on learning to teach.* East Lansing, MI: College of Education, Michigan State University.

National Center for Research on Teacher Learning (1999). *Learning from mentors.* East Lansing, MI: College of Education, Michigan State University.

National Commission on Teaching and America's Future. (1997). *Doing what matters most: Investing in quality teaching.* New York: NCTAF.

Odell, S. (1986). Induction support of new teachers: A functional approach. *Journal of Teacher Education, 37* (1), 26-29.

Odell, S. (1989). Developing support program for beginning teachers. In *Assisting the beginning teacher.* Reston, VA: Association of Teacher Educators.

Odell, S. & Ferraro, D. (1992). Teacher mentoring and teacher retention. *Journal of Teacher Education, 43* (3), 200-204.

Pajares, M.F. (1992). Teachers' beliefs and educational research: Cleaning up a messy construct. *Review of Educational Research, 62* (3), 307-332.

Reiman, A.J., Bostick, D., Cooper, J., & Lassiter, J. (1995). Counselor and teacher-led support groups for beginning teachers: A cognitive-developmental perspective. *Elementary School Guidance and Counseling, 30* (2), 105-117.

Reiman, A. & Thies-Sprinthall, L. (1998). *Mentoring & supervision for teacher development.* New York: Addison-Wesley Longman.

Rowe, M. B. (1986 January-February). Wait time: Slowing down may be a way of speeding up! *Journal of Teacher Education*: 43-49.

Saphier. J. & Gower, R. (1997). *The skillful teacher: Building your teaching skills.* Carlisle, MA: Research for Better Teaching.

Schon, D. (1983). *The reflective practitioner: How professionals think in action.* New York: Basic Books.

Schon, D. (1987). *Educating the reflective practitioner.* San Francisco: Jossey-Bass.

Shea, Gordon F. (1997). *Mentoring: How to develop successful mentor behaviors.* Los Altos, CA: Crisp Publications, Inc.

Shulman, L.S. (1987). Knowledge and teaching: Foundations of the new reform. *Harvard Educational Review, 57* (1), 1-22.

Sprinthall, N., Reiman, A. & Thies-Sprinthall, L. (1993). Roletaking and reflection: Promoting the conceptual and moral development of teachers. *Learning and individual differences, 5* (4), 283-299.

Swanson, H.L., O'Connor, J.E. & Cooney, J.B. (1990). An information processing analysis of expert and novice teachers' problem-solving. *American Educational Research Journal, 27* (3), 533-556.

Sylwester, R. (2000). *A biological brain in a cultural classroom: Applying biological research to classroom management.* Thousand Oaks, CA: Corwin Press, Inc.

Tschannen-Moran, M., Hoy, A.W. & Hoy, W.K. (1998). Teacher efficacy: Its meaning and measure. *Review of educational research, 68* (2), 202-248.

Thies-Sprinthall, L. & Gerier, E. (1990). Support groups for novice teachers. *Journal of Staff Development, 11* (4), 18-22.

U.S. Department of Education. National Center for Education Statistics. (1994b). *Qualifications of the public teacher workforce: 1988 and 1991.* Statistical Analysis Report No. 95-665, by S.A. Bobbitt and M. M. McMillen. Washington, DC: U.S. Government Printing Office.

U.S. Department of Education. National Center for Education Statistics. (1996a). *National assessment of teacher quality.* Working Paper No. 96-24, by Richard M. Ingersoll. Washington, DC: U. S. Government Printing Office.

U.S. Department of Education. National Center for Education Statistics. (1996b). *Out-of-field teaching and educational quality.* Statistical Analysis Report No. 96-040, by Richard M. Ingersoll. Washington, DC: U.S. Government Printing Office.

U.S. Department of Education. National Center for Education Statistics. (1997). *America's teachers: Profile of a profession, 1993-94.* NCES 97-460, by R. R. Henke, S. P. Choy, X. Chen, S. Geis, M. N. Alt, and S.P. Broughman. Washington, DC: U.S. Government Printing Office.

U.S. Department of Education. National Center for Education Statistics (1998a). *The TIMSS videotape classroom study: Methods and findings from an exploratory research project on eighth-grade mathematics instruction in Germany, Japan, and the United States.* Research and Development Report No. 98-047, by James W. Stigler, Patrick Gonzales, Takako Kawanaka, Steffen Knoll, and Ana Serrano. Washington, DC: U.S. Government Printing Office.

Veenman, S. (1984). Perceived problems of beginning teachers. *Review of Educational Research, 54* (2), 143-178.

Wenglinsky, H. (2000). *How teaching matters: Bringing the classroom back into discussions of teacher quality.* Princeton, NJ: Educational Testing Service.

Online Resources

The following links are offered for your review and information. They do not necessarily represent the authors' views or endorsement. Please let us know if any of these links are especially valuable, or are no longer accessible.

American Federation of Teachers--www.aft.org
   A variety of print and on-line resources for mentors and their beginning teachers.

Beginning Teacher's ToolBox—http://www.inspiringteachers.com
   Includes an 'Ask Our Mentor a Question' section, "Tips for New Teachers," and the Beginning Teachers Message Board.

Center for Cognitive Coaching—http://www.cognitivecoaching.cc
   The exclusive site for information about Cognitive Coaching[sm], including trainers' profiles, events and products.

Eisenhower National Clearinghouse for Mathematics and Science Education– http://www.enc.org/.
   A rich array of ideas and lots of free stuff, including lesson plans, curriculum units, software, professional development opportunities and web links.

Mentor Bibliography—http://www.teachermentors.com
   Recommended reading in a variety of categories pertinent to beginning teachers and their mentors.

Mentor Support Center—http://www.teachers.net
Chatboards in category-specific chats such as beginning teachers.

National Board for Professional Teaching Standards. What teachers should know and be able to do. http://www.nbpts.org

National Education Association—www.nea.org
A variety of resources and current research on teaching and induction including:
A Better Beginning: Helping new teachers survive and thrive—http://www.nea.org/teachershortage/betterbeginnings.html A guide for creating support systems for new teachers.
The NEA Foundation for Improvement in Education--http://www.nfie.org/publications/mentoring.htm. News and publications including extensive and current information on creating a teacher mentoring program.

The New Teacher Center, University of California Santa Cruz
http://www.newteachercenter.org
Multiple resources for mentors and beginning teachers including a free newsletter and other full-text resources.

Promising Practices: New Ways to Improve Teacher Quality http://www.ed.gov/pubs/PromPractices/ which includes a full chapter on The Induction of New Teachers

Questia--http://www.questia.com. A comprehensive on-line library of available print resources on mentoring, including books and journal articles.

U.S. Department of Education--www.ed.gov/index.jsp
A wealth of resources targeted for induction programs, including: The Survival Guide for New Teachers--http://www.ed.gov/pubs/survivalguide/ Ideas to new teachers effective work with veteran colleagues, parents, principals and teacher educators.
The New Teacher's Guide to the U.S. Department of Education—http://oeri.ed.gov/pubs/TeachersGuide/
Guide to finding useful information from the U.S. Dept. of Education. What to Expect Your First Year of Teaching—http://www.ed.gov/pubs/FirstYear A guide for mentors to share with their protégés, full of tips, tricks and a "help-desk" of resources and a free on-line book containing award winning first years teachers' experiences.

Index

Professional Development Programs and Services

Put Theory Into Practice In Your Schools

MiraVia offers learning-focused professional development programs and services that provide productive strategies, practical resources and innovative ideas for thoughtful educators grappling with critical professional issues.

We present workshops, seminars, and consulting services in two primary strands; Classroom Practices and Collaborative Practices. The Pathways Learning Model is a foundation for both strands.This comprehensive, research and practice-based model is a coherent framework for both student and adult learning. Applications in each strand reinforce and amplify the value of learning-focused environments and develop the individual and organizational capacities necessary to create them. This integrating quality brings a comprehensive and coherent approach to both classroom and collegial practice.

Select from the following to create the program that best meets your needs:

Classroom Practice
- Pathways to Understanding: Patterns & Practices in the Learning Focused Classroom 📖
- Pathways to Literacy: Reading and Writing in the Content Areas
- Thinking to Learn: Learning to Think
- Getting Started: Getting Smarter: Tools for Beginning Teachers

Collaborative Practices
- Data-Driven Dialogue 📖
- Mentoring Matters 📖
- Improving Student Achievement Through Learning-Focused Supervision
- The Facilitators Toolkit: Getting Work Done Together
- Enhancing Teacher Leadership: Templates and Tools for Productive Collegial Interactions

📖 Based on our book of the same title

MiraVia offers seminars in a variety of formats to best meet client needs and outcomes:

Awareness Sessions: One – Two days
Foundation Seminars: Four – Six days
Advanced Seminars: Two – Four days

We tailor consulting services,including school improvement planning, and project design to meet specific client requirements.

To learn more about these programs or to schedule a seminar for your school or district contact:

Laura Lipton, Ed.D
3 Lost Acre Trail
Sherman, CT 06784
Phone 860 354-4543
Fax 860 354-6740
lelipton@miravia.com

Bruce Wellman, M.Ed
229 Colyer Road
Guilford, VT 05301
Phone 802 257-4892
Fax 802 257-2403
bwellman@miravia.com

Go to www.miravia.com to check the calendar section for up-to-date information on conference and workshop appearances.

About the Authors

Laura Lipton, Ed.D, Co-Director of *MiraVia, LLC*
Laura Lipton is an instructional strategist who specializes in curriculum and instructional design to promote thinking, learning and thoughtful assessment. Her broad teaching background includes K-12 general and special education and teacher preparation courses. Dr. Lipton has extensive experience in literacy development, curriculum, thinking skills development, thoughtful assessment and Learning-Focused Mentoring. She leads workshops and seminars throughout the United States, Canada, Europe, Australia and New Zealand.

Contact Laura at:
3 Lost Acre Trail • Sherman, CT • 06784
P: **860.354.4543** • *F:* **860.354.6740** • *e-mail:* **lelipton@miravia.com**

Bruce Wellman, M.Ed, Co-Director of *MiraVia, LLC.*
Bruce Wellman consults with school systems, professional groups and publishers throughout the United States and Canada, presenting workshops and courses for teachers and administrators on teaching methods and materials, thinking skills development, Learning-Focused Mentoring, presentation skills and facilitating collaborative groups. Mr. Wellman has served as a classroom teacher, curriculum coordinator and staff developer in the Oberlin, Ohio, and Concord, Massachusetts, public schools. He holds a B.A. degree from Antioch College and an M.Ed from Lesley College.

Contact Bruce at:
229 Colyer Road • Guilford, VT • 05301
P: **802.257.4892** • *F:* **802.257.2403** • *e-mail:* **bwellman@miravia.com**

Carlette Humbard, M.Ed
Carlette Humbard is currently Division Manager for Harcourt School Publishers. She consults with educators at all levels in designing and implementing educational products and services. Ms. Humbard has served as a classroom educator for 15 years in addition to designing and implementing a growth-oriented teacher evaluation system for the state of Tennessee, where she served as Director of Systems Development. She has extensive experience in curriculum development, meaningful assessment, teaching methods, thinking skills development, teacher induction and Cognitive Coaching[sm].

Contact Carlette at:
7103 Ashland Glen Lakewood Ranch • Bradenton, FL • 34202
P: **407.616.1785** • *e-mail:* **chumbard@harcourt.com**

About **MiraVia**®   The Road to Learning

mira (L.)[MIR-â]: wonderful/amazing   via (L.)[VE-â]: way or road

IN 1596, the German astronomer Fabricus saw a third magnitude star in the constellation Cetus, the Whale. As they continued to observe it over the next century, astronomers became aware of its unusual fluctuations, now brighter, now fading, and honored it with the name Mira, the Wonderful.

As a partnership dedicated to continued development for professionals, we connect the constancy of presence and fluctuating brightness with the learning process. We believe that learning means working through the temporary dullness of not knowing, while pursuing the brilliance of new understanding. Our name, and our philosophy, combines this wonder of learning, Mira, with Via, or the road. Our publications, products and seminars offer pathways to professional insight and growth.